# STEP-BY-STEP
# WEEKEND
# CRAFTS

# STEP-BY-STEP
# WEEKEND
# CRAFTS

*Over 100 stylish designs and practical projects*

STAMPING *Juliet Bawden*

DOUGH CRAFT *Moira Neal*

DECOUPAGE *Juliet Bawden*

FLOWER CRAFTS *Coral Walker*

PAINTING GLASS *Moira Neal and Lynda Howarth*

NEW HOLLAND

First published in 1999 by
New Holland Publishers (UK) Ltd
24 Nutford Place, London W1H 6DQ
London · Cape Town · Sydney · Auckland

24 Nutford Place
London W1H 6DQ
United Kingdom

80 McKenzie Street
Cape Town  8001
South Africa

Level 1, Unit 4
14 Aquatic Drive
Frenchs Forest, NSW 2086
Australia

Unit 1A, 218 Lake Road
Northcote, Auckland
New Zealand

2  4  6  8  10  9  7  5  3  1

ISBN 1 85974 280 7

**Designer:** Peter Crump
**Photographer:** Shona Wood
**Editors:** Emma Callery and Gillian Haslam
**Editorial Co-ordinator:** Anke Ueberberg

**Editorial Direction:** Yvonne McFarlane

Reproduction by PICA Colour Separation, Singapore

Printed and bound in Malaysia by Times Offset (M) Sdn. Bhd.

# CONTENTS

Introduction . . . . .6

## STAMPING 8

## DOUGH CRAFT 34

## DECOUPAGE 76

## FLOWER CRAFTS 112

## PAINTING GLASS 142

# INTRODUCTION

There is something wonderfully addictive about creating a new object or decorating a piece which looks worn and tired to give it a new style, colour or pattern. Whether as a gift or as a personal item, hand-crafted and decorated items take little effort to make yet provide enormous pleasure. Many people believe that crafts require extensive artistic skills, specialist and expensive equipment, and lots of time and energy, but this is not so. This fabulous collection of projects for five versatile crafts – Stamping, Dough Craft, Decoupage, Flower Crafts and Painting Glass – requires no more than some basic tools and materials, a little imagination and a lot of enthusiasm.

*Step-by-Step Weekend Crafts* includes a wonderful range of projects that can generally be achieved within a few hours and can be assembled on the kitchen table, using many household items. Whether you wish to learn a new craft or whether you have dabbled in crafts before, this bumper book of innovative projects has something to offer for all levels of experience and will inspire you to try new techniques and make up your own designs.

Most importantly, all the crafts featured here are made accessible by full step-by-step instructions and photographs, extensive "Getting Started" sections which explain tools and techniques used in the projects, and a range of templates at the back of the book to make the projects easy to recreate. If you ever run out of ideas, the gallery pages will demonstrate dozens of additional designs for you to experiment with.

# STAMPING

Stamping is an ideal weekend craft. You need very little in the way of equipment and it takes up little or no room. In fact, everything you need can be kept in a shoe box. It has become very popular in recent years and the paints, pens, pigments, embossing powders and stamps available are continually increasing. Because the hobby has become so popular, it means that stamps are readily available everywhere, ranging from tourist shops to toy emporiums and craft stores. However, making your own stamps has the advantages of being cheaper and unique. Among other things, they can be made from sponge, foam rubber, cork, vegetables, wood and linoleum, and at the beginning of this book I will show you how to use each of these materials (see pages 10-15).

The variety of artefacts to stamp upon is enormous and ranges from interiors including walls, floors and furniture to smaller-scale items such as boxes and other containers. In addition, you can stamp on clothing and accessories.

The art of stamping is taking a block with a pattern cut into or onto it, coating it with paint and then transferring the colour and pattern onto a background. It takes a bit of practice to get the knack of how much colour to apply and how hard to press the stamp. For example, you need to apply different amounts of pressure on, say, cloth as opposed to paper. Curved surfaces are more difficult, but not impossible to stamp, and stamps will slide on a shiny glazed surface. However, a brief bit of practice on these surfaces will soon mean that you are stamping with the best of them.

The beauty of this form of decorative paint technique is that the surfaces on which you can stamp need very little or no preparation whatsoever. The only surface that may need treating is bare wood which should be cleaned and sanded before stamping on it, as with any other type of painting. The other thing to check on is that you have the right type of paint for the surface on which you are stamping — so, use fabric paints, say, on items of clothing, and emulsion paint on wooden furniture or other wooden items (see also page 15). Apart from these small points, there really is nothing to stop you from starting stamping today.

From the moment that I started writing this book, any time anyone came into the work room they had to join in. Stamping is a completely compulsive activity, and great fun, too.

Happy stamping!

Juliet Bawden

# GETTING STARTED

*Simply designed stamps can be made with everyday objects so should you want to have a go today, find a potato, a knife and some felt-tipped pens and make a start. However, many stamps with more elaborate or detailed designs are also manufactured, giving you a wide range of styles from which to choose.*

## THE HISTORY OF STAMPING

Stamps and seals have been used for thousands of years and there still exist examples which can be cited such as a Babylonian seal from 4000BC, and from 3000BC a seal from Syria (or Ebla as it was then known). Before the twentieth century, the majority of people were unable to read or write and so seals were a convenient way to authenticate documents or letters. When one person wished to communicate with another, and could not write, a scribe would be employed to write the document and the author would then present their seal which would be stamped onto the material on which the missive was written. Every person would have a personal seal which was difficult to copy. Merchants would have a picture of their trade, while others had something representative of their occupation, and naturally there are examples of stamps using script in a decorative way.

The Chinese and Japanese still use seals more frequently than most other races, as they have done for thousands of years. This may be because the script used by these nationalities lends itself naturally to seal designs. There are examples that can be seen today from Ancient Egypt and from Roman times in the British Museum. The Papal Bull is, in fact, a lead seal.

Seals and stamps were made from a variety of materials such as stone, wood, ivory and metals, even gold or silver, and many of the original, oldest examples were made from clay or bone. Seals were also formed in a variety of shapes ranging from rectangular and square to oval and circular. The round shape still remains the most popular today. Many seals were cylindrical when all script was cuniform, as in the ancient languages of Mesopotamia and Persia. The seal was used by rolling it onto the surface of clay, which was then allowed to dry in the sun. Sometimes these slabs of clay would then be enclosed, like the letter of today, into an envelope — but at that time, the envelope would be made from clay as well.

Stamps used to be placed directly onto the surface of the document but gradually it evolved and seals were placed onto softened wax. Nowadays, wax seals are used on documents to give them a mark of officialdom but many ancient papers still survive where this method was used by people who often could not write despite eminent positions of authority. In fact, seals were sometimes preferred to inked signatures because of this official appearance. Most wealthy people would have their own signet rings which would be placed into the sealing wax and this was a common way of sealing envelopes and scrolls during the eighteenth and nineteenth centuries.

Today, stamps are often made from rubber. Placed straight onto paper, they are used for many different purposes — in offices, libraries, and for many official tasks. In the last decade there has been an upsurge in the variety of rubber stamps available for decorative purposes and for use by children at home. This book illustrates how to make stamps from rubber as well as from a variety of other materials such as polystyrene, linoleum, synthetic foam, fruit, torn newspaper, and sponges, as well as using more traditional wood and metal blocks.

## SELECTING A MANUFACTURED STAMP

A traditional rubber stamp is made in three parts. The design (die) is cut from rubber, and this is laid onto a wooden handle (block) with a layer of foam (cushion) sandwiched between. When buying a rubber stamp it is worth checking certain features to make sure the stamp is easy to use and, most importantly, that the image will be clear once printed.

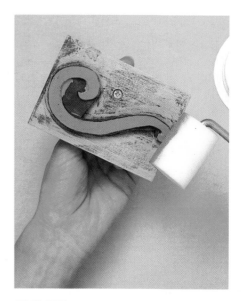

THE DIE
* Ensure that the design has been cut evenly and deeply. Those that are quite shallow will not produce a clear image, and those that are uneven will result in parts of the image not appearing. Whatever the material used for the design, it should be trimmed as closely to the edge of the design as possible.
* Some manufacturers produce polymer stamps which enable far more intricate designs to be realised. The advantage of this type of stamp is that fabric and acrylic paints are easily washed off with water, but the slight drawback is that

marker pens are not always successful.
* One other material used to make stamps is hardened plastic which can be quickly and efficiently inked. But they do not allow for any highly detailed design to be inscribed.

## THE BLOCK
* It is very difficult to produce a clear print just by holding onto the design, so the handle is very important. It should not be overly large as there will then be a temptation to rock the stamp while printing resulting in an uneven or smeared image.
* Blocks can be made from a variety of materials but be wary of those made with soft materials such as foam or sponge. There might be a tendency to push down too much which will squash both the block and the design, again causing fuzziness.

## THE CUSHION
* The cushions can either be trimmed to the shape of the outline of the design or they must be the same shape as the handle. When pressure is applied, check that it is only the design that touches the surface and not the lower edge of the handle. The depth of the cushion should therefore be checked before buying a stamp.

## MOUNTING ADHESIVE
* The three parts of the stamp are held together with adhesive which is usually a rubber cement or a mounting film. Because inks are solvent-based and so will destroy the adhesive, eventually resulting in the stamp falling apart, cleaning stamps is important. Water-based products, such as some marker pens, cannot do any damage.

## CARE OF STAMPS

1 To ensure that the die stays in good condition, always store all stamps with their rubber side down.
2 Some inks will stain the stamp even after cleaning, especially if using darker colours. However, as long as the stamp has been cleaned properly, this will not affect the quality of the print when the stamp is used again.

3 Stamps must be cleaned after use and when changing the colour.
4 After using water-based products, stamp the pad onto a piece of scrap paper or kitchen towel until only a vague impression is being made and then rinse under running water.
5 After using solvent-based inks, keep stamping until as little ink as possible is left — as for water-based products — and then dry them thoroughly. This should be sufficient but, if not, use a mix of water and washing-up liquid or other detergent and gently clean. It might be useful to have an old nail brush or toothbrush which can be used if there is a really stubborn stain.
6 Always clean stamps immediately. When this is impossible, stamp on to a scrap piece of paper to remove as much ink as you can and then place the stamp on a damp sponge or towel. The ink that is left will not dry as long as it is kept wet.
7 When ink has dried onto the stamp, dab solvent-based cleaner onto the die and gently scrub with a toothbrush.
8 Never immerse the whole stamp in water as this is quite unnecessary and can actually affect the adhesive used to make the stamp.

## TOOLS AND EQUIPMENT

You will find that you already have much of the equipment needed for making stamps and for practising the art of stamping in your home. Many stamps, paints, inks, and materials on which to print can obviously be bought, but at first, it is advisable to experiment with what is already available as this will save a lot of time and expense.

## MAKING A RUBBER STAMP

For the rubber you will need:
Rubber erasers
Tracing paper
Soft pencil
Fountain pen
Needle
Craft knife
Sandpaper
Scrap paper

1 Choose a rubber of a suitable size and work out a design. White rubber is preferable, and the less springy the better. For the design, either copy one of the templates from pages 177-178, or create your own pattern or picture.
2 Trace the image to be copied, or draw the design, heavily onto the tracing paper using the soft pencil. Then shade on top of all the heavier drawn lines until they are covered.
3 Turn the tracing paper over and hold it firmly in place on top of the rubber. Draw heavily on top of the lines of the design and this will then be transferred to the top of the rubber.
4 Use the fountain pen to go over the image, correcting any missed parts. The reversed image can now be seen more clearly, so making it easier to see while cutting out.
5 Slowly stroke the needle over the outline several times, allowing the surface of the rubber to be cut just a miniscule amount. Don't score a line immediately — just stroke gently. The angle of this initial scoring should be away from the image with no undercutting.
6 Now use the tip of a very sharp craft knife and cut the lines of the image a little deeper taking care to keep the angle of the cut sloping. The cut-away section should narrow towards the top like a sand dune.
7 Clean any excess ink from the rubber with a moistened tissue or baby wipe. Then place the stamp onto an ink pad and take a first print onto a smooth piece of paper. You will then be able to see where rough edges need to be trimmed and to generally check that the image is correct.
8 Trim excess rubber and any rough areas with the knife and then take another print to check. Repeat this process until a clear, satisfactory image is achieved. If there are any large areas in the design it may help to keep these clear by making deeper cuts in the rubber with the knife.
9 If small mistakes are not too deep, they can be corrected by using sandpaper to rub down the surface. If it is not possible to rectify an image, use the other side of the rubber and start again. Alternatively, if a rubber is large

enough, cut it into smaller sections or remove one part of a design if a mistake has been made.

For the block you will need:
Wood or dowelling to suit the stamp
Small saw
5 mm (¼ in)-thick cellulose sponge
Adhesive

1 Cut a suitable length of wood or dowelling to fit the back of the stamp. This should not overlap the stamp but it can be the same size or slightly smaller. It would be impossible to place the stamp accurately if the block is larger than the stamp, as the stamp cannot be seen if this happens.
2 Cut the cellulose sponge to the same shape as the stamp and then glue this to the back of the rubber stamp.
3 Next, glue the wooden handle to the back of the sponge.
4 Make a mark on the stamp or the handle to indicate which is the top of the image.

The stamp does not necessarily need a handle, but it is much easier to use and less messy if there is something to hold other than the stamp. Many offices have stamps which are no longer used, so if you can obtain some of these the

rubber can be stripped from the handle and the handle reused. Hoarded or waste objects such as cotton reels, small jars with lids, and plastic boxes, can also be used as handles.

For a more professional finish, either stamp the image onto the back of the handle or onto a piece of paper which is then glued onto the handle. Give it three coats of varnish and, when dry, glue the handle onto the rubber stamp.

## STAMPS MADE USING OTHER MATERIALS

As long as the stamping medium will adhere to it, you can use any object as a stamp, whatever the shape or size, plain or patterned. Indian shops are a source of old fabric stamps; metal and wooden stamps can be sought from printers; biscuit cutters are a useful pre-cut tool, and patterned rubber rollers from decorators' outlets can be used, especially if a larger area needs to be covered. Inca-wheels (roller stamps that produce a continuous pattern) can be found in many shops nowadays, and make good presents for children as they are easy to use. They often have interchangeable wheels so you can quickly vary the designs.

### CORK

Cork can be bought in sheets of varying thicknesses or you can simply use cork matting. Transfer a design onto the cork surface in the same way as above, and then using a sharp craft knife, gradually cut out the image. Corks from bottles can also be used as stamping tools, either as circular stamps which will leave a patterned impression from the corks or a design can be cut from the side or top and the corks used in this way. Draw a design on the cork in pen or pencil ① and then carefully cut it out with a craft knife ②. The design should be fairly simple as the cork can be fiddly to cut away. You can also buy more detailed cork stamps ③.

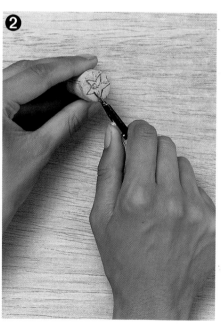

## LINOLEUM

Linoleum is readily available from craft shops in standard sizes and it can be cut into different shapes with strong scissors. Draw your design directly onto the surface with a pencil which can be easily erased with a rubber. Specialist cutting tools can be bought from craft suppliers and there are numerous different shaped blades available. These are interchangeable so you need only purchase one handle. For information on making a lino cut, see the lino-cut bird on pages 18-19.

Once you are happy with your design, cut around it with the cutting tool ④. Then neaten the linoleum by trimmimg around the stamp with a sharp pair of scissors ⑤. Cover the image with an even coat of paint ⑥, and finally stamp ⑦.

## FRUIT AND VEGETABLES

Fresh produce can be used for printing with the most wonderful results. There are innumerable fruits and vegetables that can be used, such as apples, lemons, hard plums, potatoes, turnips and carrots. When using the fruit or vegetable for its own imprint, citrus fruits and apples produce particularly interesting prints.

When cutting into the surface to create a pattern it is better to use a potato or other vegetable with a hard inner surface. Lino cutting tools can be used for gouging out the image required and, as stated above, there are many different blades available. Dried fruit

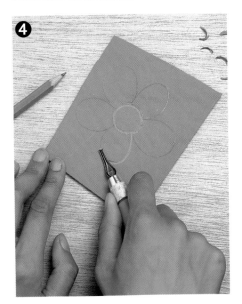

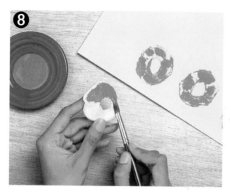

To cut a stamp from a piece of sponge first draw the design onto a piece of sponge using a felt tipped pen ⑭. Then carefully cut it out using scissors ⑮.

can also be used such as apple rings and pears ⑧. An interesting shape is particularly good for repeat patterns. To make a potato print, first clean the potato thoroughly and then cut it in half ⑨. Draw the shape onto the cut side of the potato using a felt-tipped pen ⑩. Then, using a craft knife, cut away the part of the design you do not want printed, so that the part you do want stands proud of the surface ⑪. Finally, paint colour onto the part standing proud and then print onto your surface ⑫.

## POLYSTYRENE

Polystyrene trays that fresh meat and fish are placed in at supermarkets make excellent surfaces from which to print. A pencil, twig or any blunt tool can be used to make a picture or pattern on the polystyrene surface from which a print can then be taken. This is particularly successful with children who can create quite complicated patterns easily on this surface.

You can buy polystyrene ceiling or wall tiles that are often already patterned. The pattern can be used exactly as it is, or it can be cut into to make an image incorporating the pattern already in place ⑬.

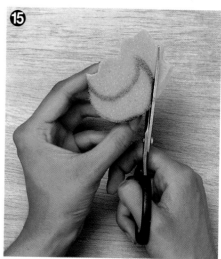

## SPONGE

Sponges come in pre-cut shapes or you can cut out the shape required from a sheet of sponge. It is easier to use thin sponge as thicker ones tend to be rather messy. To get a good print from sponge it is best to apply only a thin layer of ink and not to press too hard.
It is also possible to use compressed sponge, but be careful about allowing this to become wet as it will expand. It is best to mount compressed sponge on a handle.

## SCRUNCHED PAPER

Scrunched and torn paper make interesting impressions when used as stamps. Whole walls in rooms have been printed in this way, yet at the other end of the scale, wonderful cards and wrapping papers can also be created using this method of stamping.

## WOOD

Wood can be carved to make a die though it should be noted that wooden stamps are more successful if the image stands out from the block as opposed to being indented. It is difficult to produce a clear image if it is indented because of the nature of the material.

You can buy a variety of wooden stamps from many outlets — and wooden stamps that newspaper and magazine printers used are often to be found in antique and junk shops.

# STAMPING MEDIUM

The surface on which you are going to stamp determines the kind of ink that will be used. Most fluids can be used as inks as long as they can be applied to the die and will adhere to the material on which the stamp is to be placed. Traditionally, you would buy an ink pad inked with a pre-selected colour and once the pad is dry it can be re-inked. However, a whole variety of media can now be used and is readily available so consult the lables on all containers to see what is the most appropriate product for your project.

### INK
Inks can be permanent on non-permanent and this should be noted when purchasing the product. It is always easier to use a stamp pad for these inks ① and it is possible to make one using layers of felt covered with muslin. This should be placed in a container with a lid which will keep the pad damp, preventing the ink from drying up. Bottles of ink are available from stationers and art suppliers in a multitude of colours. The pads are best stored upside down to keep the ink at the surface.

### FELT-TIPPED PENS
Felt-tipped pens are produced with permanent and non-permanent inks, water-based and solvent-based. Experiment to find out which adheres

best to which materials. The advantage of using felt-tipped pens is that different areas of the design can be coloured with a variety of colours, so once stamped, a multi-coloured image will appear on the surface of the material.

### PAINTS
Most paints can be used for printing, whether they are powder, ink or poster paints ②. Usually the thicker the paint, the better the result as the colour will be more vibrant.

A wide range of emulsion paint is now available in small quantities and you can also have colours made up. This type of paint produces some wonderful effects and, again, sections of a stamp can be painted in different colours before stamping.

## GENERAL TIPS BEFORE STAMPING

1 Ensure that the work surface on which you are stamping is flat and hard.

2 Make sure that all materials on which you are printing are flat, removing creases if working with fabric and use masking tape to keep other products in place. This will help you to concentrate on the stamping rather than attempting to keep the paper or fabric still as well! When stamping onto a box, lampshade, or similar, secure the object as well as you can before starting to stamp.

3 Always test the stamp on a scrap of paper or material first as this is the only chance you will have to rectify any problems that might occur with either the die or the medium being used.

4 Do not over-ink the stamp as the result will be a smudged image. When using an ink pad, lightly tap the stamp on the surface, do not press down hard. If using a brush to apply paint, make sure it has been gently stroked along the edge of the pot before brushing onto the image and ensure that the paint is applied evenly. It is worth noting that less ink is needed when the image is finely detailed.

5 Do not rock the stamp once on the surface as the image will blur. Larger stamps need firm pressure at the centre and while held in place, lighter pressure should be applied around the edges.

6 If you are using a second colour over the first stamp, always allow plenty of time for the first set of stamps to dry.

# TERRACOTTA FLOWERPOTS

*A bright and colourful design can be made by using only one stamp with more than one colour, and by painting only part of the block, the design can be altered. The designs shown here have been stamped using very bright coloured emulsion paints - and paint was only applied to half the block.*

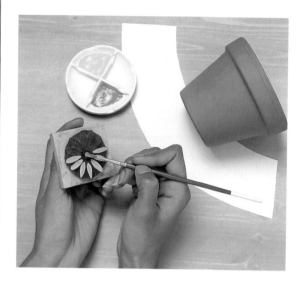

**1** Measure the circumference of each pot and make paper collars to fit around them — these will be your practice areas. Then, using the paintbrush, paint emulsion colours onto the section of the stamp that you wish to print.

## VARIATIONS

Select alternative emulsion colours for a different effect — here, we have used combinations of blue, yellow and green.

16

2 Stamp the design onto the paper template to see how it will look on the pot. If you do not like the pattern, you can try something else on another collar without making a mess of the flowerpot. If you are changing colours on the block, wash off the paint in warm water, using a nail brush to ensure all the crevices are clean; pat dry with a clean cloth and then reapply paints and try out the design once more.

3 Apply more paint to the block and, holding it firmly against the flowerpot, roll it from one side to the other without lifting it from the surface of the pot. Now lift off the stamp, being careful not to smudge the paint.

4 Turn the block through 180 degrees so that the pattern is turned around, add more paint, and repeat step 3. Continue in this way, adding more paint to the block as you go, until the base of the flowerpot is covered with the design. If necessary, neaten the stamp prints with the paintbrush.

5 For the top rims, paint just a small portion of the stamp and make a pattern around the top edge of the flowerpot to make a border. Stamp a complete daisy on the base of the pot, too, if you wish.

# WOODEN CHAIR WITH BIRD LINO PRINTS

*Lino cuts make unique stamps, and the design can be your own or copied from something that you like. The cutting made for this chair is of a little bird, which was cut to fit onto the width of the wooden slats. The effect from lino stamps is quite rough and earthy as the image is transferred in an uneven manner. But it can be touched up if you prefer a smooth finish.*

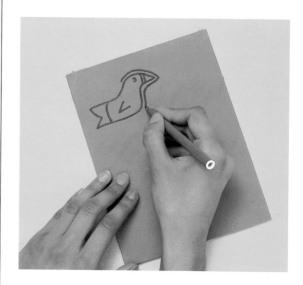

**1** Remembering that the lines you draw will be in relief once they are stamped, draw a design onto the lino with your marker pen or pencil. The simpler your design, the stronger the stamped image will be. If you want to use the same bird design, transfer the template on page 178 onto the lino.

## YOU WILL NEED

Small piece of lino

Fine marker pen (black) or a soft pencil

Bird template (page 178)

Lino cutter

Scissors or craft knife

Wooden chair

Paintbrush (fine)

Stamping paint (stone)

## VARIATIONS

You will see from the photograph to the left, that birds have also been stamped on the seat of this slatted chair. Instead of repeating this triangular pattern, perhaps you could randomly scatter the birds across the seat, or make an arrow-head shape, as if for a flock of birds in flight.

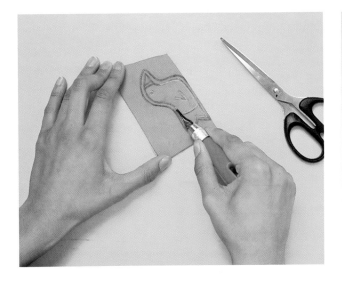

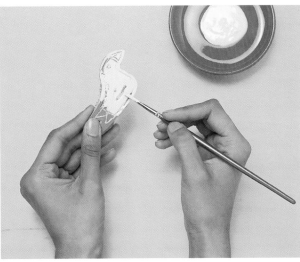

2 Carefully cut along the lines with the lino cutter. Hold the cutter firmly, with your thumb placed on the top of the handle, and push the cutter blade into the lino and push away from yourself. The lino will peel away as you do this. Then cut around the edge with the scissors or craft knife.

3 Using the paintbrush, paint the lino cutting with the stone coloured stamping paint. Make sure you don't overload the paintbrush with paint as it will make this process a little messy.

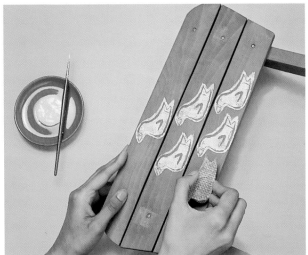

4 Place the lino cutting face down onto the chair where you wish to stamp it. Press it down firmly, especially around the edges pushing the cutting down here as they tend to rise outwards once they are damp. Lift off in one swift movement.

5 Repeat stamping to create a pattern of your choice, adding a fresh coat of paint each time. A triangular pattern like the one here is very simple and easy to do.

# GINGHAM BAG

*Gingham fabric comes in bright, cheerful colours — predominantly blue, red and yellow — and it is the ideal fabric for a children's bedroom, whether for curtains, a quilt cover or, as here, a handy bag for putting things in. The red star stamped all over it adds a very attractive decoration.*

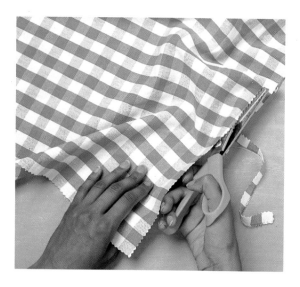

**1** Cut a piece of gingham to the width of the finished bag plus 5 cm (2 in) seam allowances, and twice the desired length. Press the fabric so that it is smooth when being stamped on.

## YOU WILL NEED

Gingham fabric

Dressmaker's scissors

Pencil

Star stamp

Paintbrush

Fabric paint (red)

Cotton thread

Ribbon

--- **VARIATIONS** ---

Make stars of all colours — don't feel obliged to stick to one colour, like here. Alternatively, stamp onto every white square but in alternate rows, leaving every other row blank.

2 To prevent confusion when printing, mark every square with a faint pencil dot where you are going to print. Do this on the right side of the fabric and then lay out the fabric ready to be stamped on.

3 Paint the fabric paint onto the motif using the paintbrush. Then place the motif above the first square where you wish the colour to be dark and carefully apply it.

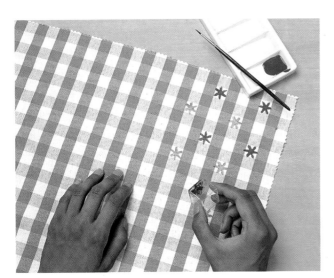

4 Without repainting the motif, stamp it into the next square. In this way you will get a pattern of light and dark motifs. Continue stamping the star across the bag in the same way.

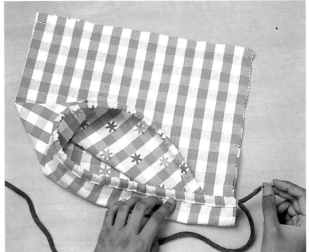

5 Make up the bag by folding it in half with the right sides together and the fold at the bottom of the bag. Then sew up the sides with a neat running stitch. At the top of the bag make a casing for the ribbon by folding over the top twice and stitching it in place leaving a gap for the ribbon to be inserted. Thread the ribbon through to finish the bag — use a safety pin at the end to help it — and finally turn the right sides out.

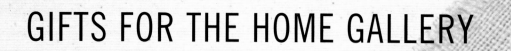

# GIFTS FOR THE HOME GALLERY

## Flowerpot
Ceramic is a difficult surface on which to stamp. It is easier to stamp onto earthenware as the stamp will not slide. On curved surfaces such as these, start with one side of the stamp and roll it over the surface and lift in one deft movement.

## Soaps
Soap can be turned into a special gift by wrapping in plain brown, green and blue paper and stamping with a shell design.

## Tiles
Bathroom tiles can either be stamped using gloss paint or with emulsion which is then given a protective coat of varnish.

## Gift box
A small plywood box has the centre of a tile stamped onto its lid and a tiny pattern stamped round its sides.

## Table mats

Easy to make table mats made from fringed hessian stamped in two shades of terracotta.

## Lampshade

A grubby lampshade has been given a new lease of life by sponging with mushroom emulsion paint, leaving it to dry before sponging gold sea horses all around the edge.

## Saucer

Unglazed ceramic takes stamps very successfully – this saucer is stamped with daisy sections.

## Picture frame

A wooden frame has been given a colourwash before being stamped with lino cuts of stars and flashes.

## Jug

A small jug is stamped on its unglazed surface using white quarter daisies with yellow centres.

# DAISY ENVELOPES

*Customize and personalize your own and your child's stationery by stamping small prints onto paper and envelopes alike. The designs can range from tiny black prints on sophisticated cartridge paper to brightly coloured daisies, like those on the envelopes stamped here.*

## YOU WILL NEED

Daisy stamp

Acrylic paints (pink, green)

Paintbrush (fine)

Plain envelopes

## VARIATIONS

On the writing paper, a border has been stamped all the way around, but it would be just as interesting to stamp down just one side, say, or along the bottom edge. The end result would be nicely understated.

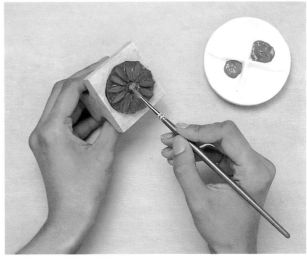

1 Holding the daisy stamp steady, carefully paint the petals using the pink acrylic paint. Use the fine paintbrush to do this as it means you will be less likely to smudge the paint.

2 Clean the paintbrush in warm water and then paint the centre of the flower with the green acrylic paint. Make sure that the paint is the right thickness for stamping, by testing the stamp on scrap paper first.

3 Decide on where you wish to stamp the daisy and press the stamp down firmly, rocking it ever so slightly from side to side to ensure that the whole image is transferred. Lift the stamp swiftly and in one smooth movement to avoid smudging.

4 You may find that the stamped image is uneven in places. If so, paint over any part of the petals or the centre that you wish to tidy up with the same paintbrush.

# GIFTS FOR ADULTS GALLERY

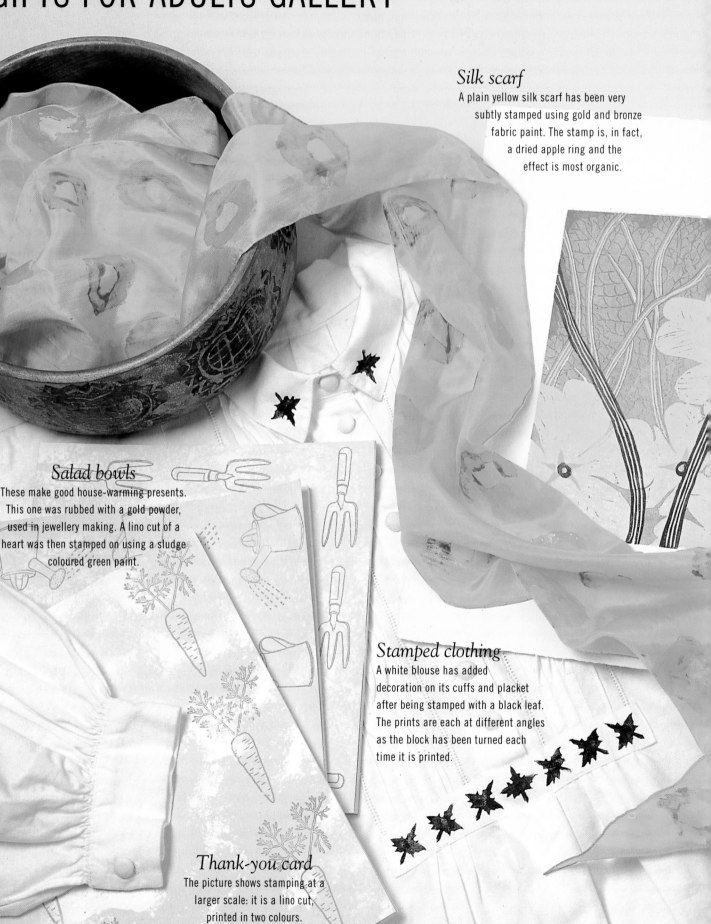

## Silk scarf
A plain yellow silk scarf has been very subtly stamped using gold and bronze fabric paint. The stamp is, in fact, a dried apple ring and the effect is most organic.

## Salad bowls
These make good house-warming presents. This one was rubbed with a gold powder, used in jewellery making. A lino cut of a heart was then stamped on using a sludge coloured green paint.

## Stamped clothing
A white blouse has added decoration on its cuffs and placket after being stamped with a black leaf. The prints are each at different angles as the block has been turned each time it is printed.

## Thank-you card
The picture shows stamping at a larger scale: it is a lino cut, printed in two colours.

## Folk art cupboard

The design on the cupboard of folk art birds and hearts has been made by building up the design using a variety of different stamps.

## Stamped shoes

Rather dull brown suede espadrilles have been decorated for a beach holiday with a stamp of a large sea shell.

## Paper lampshade

The fleur-de-lys is a popular motif and it has been used here with great effect on a paper lampshade.

# HALLOWE'EN FRIEZE

*Friezes like this are incredibly quick and simple to make — just right for a one-off occasion like Hallowe'en. For large designs like this pumpkin face, a swede is the ideal vegetable for stamping with.*

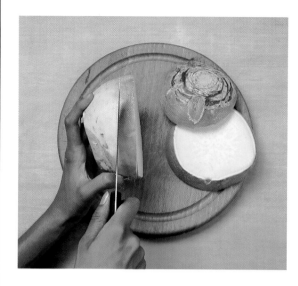

**1** Cut the swede in half. Then trace the templates on pages 177 and 178 and transfer them, one to each half of the cut swede. Do this by laying the tracing paper over the swede and cut through the lines with the craft knife.

## VARIATIONS

In place of either the pumpkin or bat, make your own witch's hat stamp — this is particularly easy to cut from a swede as it has such a simple outline.

**2** Carefully cut out the design using the craft knife. Cut around the edges first and then carefully cut out slithers of swede from the more detailed parts, such as the eyes and mouth.

**3** Cut the lining paper to the depth you would like the frieze to be and paint it orange. To achieve the above paint effect, load the paintbrush with paint and then dip it in some water before transferring it onto the lining paper. In this way the degrees of colour intensity will vary. Leave the paint to dry.

**4** First stamp on the pumpkin images. Using the black paint, paint the pumpkin face on the swede and then stamp along the frieze. Add paint to the swede between each stamp to retain a consistent printed image.

**5** Using black paint again, stamp the bats onto the frieze. Position them between, above and below the pumpkin faces and let them fly at different angles by rotating the swede as you stamp.

# EMBOSSED CHRISTMAS DECORATIONS

*Embossing is a stamping technique with an amazing result. Here, for a festive feel, Christmas decorations are made by embossing cartridge paper with copper and silver powder. They are then cut out to make small shapes suitable for hanging from a tree.*

**1** Using the black ink pad and either the fleur-de-lys or paisley stamps (here, we used the fleur-de-lys one), stamp the image onto the cartridge paper. Apply the ink to the stamp by tapping the stamp onto the ink pad or wiping the ink pad over the stamp.

## YOU WILL NEED

Stamping ink pad (black)

Fleur-de-lys stamp

Paisley stamp

Cartridge paper

Embossing powder (copper, silver)

Paintbrush (fine)

Heat source (iron or toaster)

Scissors

Coloured card

Glue

Hole punch

Ribbon

### — VARIATIONS —

Make gift tags in the same way but you only need to glue a single image to the coloured card so that there is space on the back for your message and name.

2 While the image is still wet, sprinkle the embossing powder (here, we used the copper powder) all over it. Shake off the excess powder onto a clean piece of paper and, if necessary, use the small paintbrush to remove any stubborn excess powder.

3 Hold the embossed cartridge paper above the heat source until the powder melts onto the paper. This will take a few minutes and the end result is a raised, metallic image.

4 To make each decoration, you will need two images, one for each side, but make sure that you have a reversible design. The paisley motifs opposite would work for one-sided decorations only. Cut around each embossed image, leaving a small border, and also cut out the coloured card to your required shape, remembering to allow a space at the top for a hole. Then glue the cut out embossed images onto both sides of the coloured card and leave to dry.

5 Using the hole punch, punch a hole into the top of the card. Then thread the ribbon through this hole, tie a knot at the top and hang the decoration on your Christmas tree, or, say, a series of them across a window.

# GIFTS FOR SPECIAL OCCASIONS GALLERY

### *Wrapping paper*
Red wrapping paper with a fibre running through it has been stamped with a heart design in gold. To make a pretty parcel it was tied with gold and red ribbon with added hearts.

### *Candles*
The candles have been stamped with a golden star design using stamping paint. When stamping on wax, it is worth experimenting with different paints as some of them will not dry and just smudge.

### *Festive napkin holders and napkins*
Suitable for parties, these can be made from cardboard tubes which are covered in a layer of papier mâché, then painted blue and stamped with a simple gold star design. Navy paper napkins have been stamped with signs of the zodiac.

### *Wrapping ribbon*
Grosgrain ribbon has been cut with pointed ends and then stamped with a heart at each end.

## Voile curtain

A voile curtain is made to look special by stamping golden suns, moons and stars all over it at random.

## Pin cushion

This pin cushion was stamped with a fleur-de-lys. It makes a pretty mother's day, or birthday present. The edges of the stamped image have been dotted with pearl beads and pins.

## Cracker

To make a mother's day wrapping paper, a rose design was cut from lino and stamped onto green paper. The present was then wrapped up to look like a cracker.

## Candle shades

These have been stamped with a repeat paisley design which fits perfectly.

# DOUGH CRAFT

Who would believe that a visit to the library for a book on creative writing could start an obsession with salt dough modelling? I walked in and there it was. A brand new book on the subject. I decided that I would give it a go and by the next day I had made my first creation: a bowl edged with fruit which was much admired.

Needless to say, the creative writing disappeared in a cloud of flour; dough had made a take-over bid for my time and kitchen. Never again was the oven cool or the kitchen clean. I was in the stranglehold of this compulsive hobby. Even while the dinner was cooking I'd quickly mix a batch of dough and rustle up a new and unique object.

Soon, I had read all there was to read on the subject but felt hungry for more. Not a day passed without an experiment into a new method of basket weaving, vegetable design, pencil top or light pull. I concluded that anything can be made from it — and, indeed, that it just what I have done; shelf upon shelf of dough-made items. I think that the moment of truth finally arrived in the supermarket the day I had seven bags of salt in my trolley and the cashier enquired if I was expecting bad weather. It then occurred to me that we, the salt dough fraternity, have seriously distorted the figures that the boffins produce about our annual consumption of basic commodities like flour and salt. Do they realise that so much is being converted into works of art (or indeed missiles should anyone dare say anything uncomplimentary about them) not body fat? Ah well… we know something they don't know!

As for dough craft being the ideal weekend pastime, well — all you need to do is delve into the depths of your kitchen cupboard for flour, salt and cooking oil, mix the lot together and you are instantly free to explore the world of modelling. Likewise, many of the modelling tools required are to be found in a kitchen drawer so you don't need to spend many days planning in advance.

Many of the ideas included in this book are extremely quick to make: a few twists of salt dough sausages here and some deft modelling of small apples and blackberries there and you instantly have a twisted autumn garland. Of course, the overnight cooking is something that can't be rushed, but once the dough is dried out, the painting and varnishing for the finishing touches really don't take many minutes. So, with modelling on a Saturday and painting on a Sunday, here is the ideal weekend activity. I hope that you get as much fun out of it as I have and whether you are already a hardened fanatic, or just starting out, there should be enough ideas in this book to fuel your enthusiasm. I need an excuse to write another!

Moira Neal

# GETTING STARTED

*The basic ingredients for making the dough and
then modelling it are few and easily obtainable.
This is what makes the craft so appealing - almost
everything you need can be found in the kitchen,
and most other items in the garden.*

## YOU WILL NEED

| |
|---|
| Apron |
| Plain flour |
| Cooking salt |
| Large mixing bowl |
| Weighing scales or measuring cups |
| Wooden spoon |
| Small container of water |
| Baking sheets |
| Lard for greasing trays |
| Aluminium foil for covering nonstick trays and for supporting dough while it is being cooked |
| Dredger |
| Rolling pin |
| Unserrated knife |
| Fork with even prongs |
| Old pencil |
| Grater |
| Card for templates |
| Scissors |
| Set of circular cutters or a selection of empty cans and bottle tops |
| Cocktail sticks (toothpicks) for indenting, texturing and supporting |
| Garlic press for hair, grass and roots |
| Drinking straws for coring out holes |
| Black peppercorns (wonderful for eyes) |
| Cloves |
| Few twigs for stalks |
| Paints |
| Paintbrushes |

| |
|---|
| Polyurethane varnish |
| Drill |
| Florist's stub wire for hanging projects: thicker gauge wire for large projects (wire coat hangers are ideal for this), paper clips for hanging smaller models |
| Wire cutters |
| Pliers |
| Two-part epoxy resin or hot glue gun |
| Craft glue |

### USEFUL BUT NOT ESSENTIAL

| |
|---|
| Biscuit cutters (handy for making refrigerator magnets and small decorations) |
| Brooch backs, magnets and earring findings if you wish to make refrigerator magnets and jewellery |
| Cake icing cutters (these really speed up production and quickly pay for themselves) |
| Cardboard roll for napkin rings |
| Clip frames |
| Clock movement |
| Modelling tools |
| Nylon icing bag and nozzles |
| Potato ricer for simulating rag doll hair and willow |
| Small piece of nylon netting for making texture |

If you do not have a good selection of baking trays and dishes, take a few trips to your local car boot or jumble sale. It always pays to fill the oven each time you make dough. If you want to make picture frames, buy old frames and use the glass, and you can also pick up mirrors of all sizes which can easily be converted into works of art.

ADDITIONS FROM NATURE

It is always fun to have an excuse to go for a walk or take a trip to the seaside and salt dough provides one. The autumn is the time to collect beech nut cases, fir cones of all sizes and seed heads. Also make a collection of twigs to be used for stalks in place of cloves if you wish. A beach walk will provide shells (make sure they are empty first), tumbled glass, driftwood, stones and seaweed, all of which can be wetted and pushed into the dough. Old nuts left over from Christmas also make unusual additions and the cracked outer shells of pistachio nuts make wonderful mouse ears! If you have a bowl of pot pourri, you may well find an interesting collection of tropical seed heads and cones that may also be used.

MAKING SALT DOUGH

The following ingredients make one batch of dough, as refered to in the projects in this book. Use weighing scales or a set of cup measures.

270 g (2 level cups) plain flour
320 g (1 level cup) cooking salt
180 ml (¾ cup) water
10 ml (2 tsp) cooking oil (optional)

1 Measure the dry ingredients. If you are using cups, fill each cup to the top and levelling it off with a knife. Take care not to pack down the ingredients.

2 Mix the ingredients together and then add the water, again filling the measure right to the top. Bind the ingredients together, turn out onto a work surface and knead for 10 minutes. (A food mixer with a dough hook is ideal for this and really helps to produce a good workable dough.) It is important to knead the dough for the full 10 minutes as it develops the gluten content and makes the dough easier to work with. To check that it is ready, roll a small amount into a ball and it should not crack. It should also feel firm and slightly tacky. Add more water very gradually if needed.

3 If you find that you need much more water than the quantity stipulated here, change to a different brand of flour. Too much water makes the dough less workable and it takes longer to cook. Once you have found a make of flour and salt that work well for you, stick to them and you will find it easier to get consistently good results.

4 Some people advocate the use of cooking oil and wallpaper paste in their dough but the above dough should work very well without the oil added. If, however, you find the dough difficult to work, add the cooking oil; it will help prevent the dough from sticking to your hands and is recommended if you are working with children.

## COLOURING DOUGH
This is a great technique for those who do not like painting and is ideal for children as the only finishing needed is two coats of varnish. Food colours are ideal for this purpose when light fastness is not a problem, and may be added either as the dough is being made or kneaded in afterwards. If a complete batch is to be coloured, dissolve the colour in the water before adding to the

dry ingredients. Use liquid paints or gouache for a more light fast finish. Mix them in by taking small quantities of the dough. Roll them out flat, add a little colour in the middle, fold over and then knead the dough until the colour is evenly distributed throughout ①.

It is also possible to use natural ingredients to colour dough, and coffee (dissolve first in a spot of boiling water), cocoa, paprika and spices are all ideal ②. Hang the finished model out of direct sunlight for longer-lasting

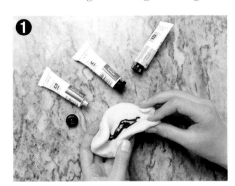

colour. For a variety of colours, make up the dough first and then divide and colour as required and keep each colour in a separate bag.

Alternatively, for a rustic effect, use a selection of different flours. In this book, buckwheat has been used for some of the leaves on the natural dough wreath (see pages 58) together with rye flour for a paler effect. The doughs were made in the same way as basic dough, but substituting the chosen flour for the plain flour. More or less water may be needed to get the consistency right and, as buckwheat flour is gluten free, it is quite fragile to work with. The made-up dough for both buckwheat and rye will keep for weeks stored in an airtight container.

## PREPARING BAKING TRAYS
Lightly grease baking trays with lard to ensure the safe removal of your model. Non-stick trays tend to mark the back of the dough and so it is worth covering them with aluminium foil first.

---

### TIPS FOR SUCCESS

• Always knead your dough for at least ten minutes.

• Keep ready-made dough covered and use within a few hours of making for the best results. It starts to become floppy as the salt dissolves and may be unmanageable by the next day. It is possible to reknead for ten minutes with the addition of more flour, but for the effort involved, it is as well to start from scratch.

• Stick dough together using water, either with a small paintbrush, or use your finger. Avoid wetting the surface of dough which is not to be painted as it will mark during baking. Any nuts, twigs or other bits you are adding to your model should be wet before positioning. Should they come loose during baking, secure with glue once the model has cooled. You may prefer to make up a little dough paste to use as a gluing agent if your dough is slightly dry, and this is done by adding water, a little at a time until you have achieved a mushy consistency.

• If you have dough left over at the end of a project why not rustle up some of the small ideas shown in this book which you can use to fill the spaces on your baking tray? Alternatively, make some spare leaves, fruits and flowers to practise painting on.

• If you have a really large project in mind, measure the internal dimensions of your oven (avoiding the back to allow free air circulation) and buy or have made a suitable sized baking sheet; sides are not required remember. I have found that aluminium is the best metal for baking on.

• Bake dough as soon as you have finished modelling it. If it is left to air dry first, the surface becomes crumbly and any unsupported leaves tend to break off easily. When dough is baked in the oven a chemical change takes place which strengthens the finished model.

# MODELLING TECHNIQUES

The key thing to know about salt dough is that when you are sticking anything together, whether it be strips for basket weave, or fruit and vegetables to decorate, you should always use water. It acts just like glue.

## TEXTURING SALT DOUGH

All manner of household items can be used for printing texture and it is worth building up a collection of buttons, pieces of lace, wood and cake icing embossing tools. The more you look around, the more ideas you will have.

Use scissors to make a fur or feather effect. For fur, make tiny snips into the dough varying the angle all the time. For feathers, make even rows of V-snips following the natural line of feathers. This method can also be used for texturing trees, making hedgehog spines, and for making ears of wheat ①.

To give a woolly texture, grate the dough. Then carefully pick up the grated dough using tweezers and place on the wet dough model ②. This gives a fragile finish, but it is fine for a wall decoration which is not going to be disturbed.

## MAKING BASKET WEAVES

There are a great number of possibilities here but the simplest effect comes from using a fork. Choose one with even, equally spaced prongs and use regular pressure as you push it into the dough. There are three variations shown below ①.

Alternatively, start with a rolled slab of dough and then apply strips of rope. Work in one direction first and then the other ②. Cut off any overhanging strips with a sharp knife. The thinner the strips, the more delicate the effect.

To make a coarser, woven wood style of weave, again start with a slab of dough and cover it with strips of thinly rolled dough, weaving them together as you stick them to the base ③.

## MAKING A TRELLIS

A trellis can either be made using a lattice pie cutter (such as some of the baskets in the gallery on pages 52-53), or for a more freehand feel, stick together strips of dough, working first in one direction diagonally, and then overlapping the stripes in the other ①.

## PIPING DOUGH

One of the most exciting aspects of using salt dough is experimenting with new modelling techniques. Piping is a quick and very creative way to model salt dough and a nylon piping bag is the best thing to use as it holds a lot of dough and is re-usable. Among its other uses, use piping for adding features to faces, tendrils to ivy, and writing names and messages. It is also useful as a glue to stick larger pieces together and the consistency can be altered accordingly.

To make the dough a suitable consistency for piping, take a small quantity of dough and mix with water until it is mushy. You may need to experiment to get a pipeable consistency. If required, add food colouring or gouache paints at this stage (see page 37). Place a piping nozzle (nos 2 or 3) in a nylon piping bag, add the dough and treat as icing.

Similar effects can be achieved using a clay gun and with its large number of discs other effects may also be found, but you will probably not need to add any more water to the dough.

## MAKING HAIR

A garlic press is useful for making hair as well as vegetable roots and any length may be obtained by opening the press and reloading with dough. A sieve or fine netting may also be used for making fine strands.

A potato ricer is another interesting gadget to use with the dough. Put a small quantity of dough in at a time, cover with a piece of baking parchment and squeeze. Refill the ricer until the dough is the right length. The parchment will enable you to open the ricer more easily. Riced dough makes wonderful rag doll style hair and can also be used to make willow wreaths and garlands.

## MAKING A DOUGH ROPE
If you were a whiz with modelling dough when you were little, making a smooth, even rope will come easily to you, but others may find it surprisingly difficult. The dough must be very well kneaded to make a successful rope. Roll the dough lightly using your fingers but if you have trouble making a smooth rope, roll with a baking tray instead of your hands.

To make a twisted rope, make two identical lengths and lay one rope diagonally across the other. Starting in the centre, work towards one end, alternately flipping one piece over the other. Repeat for the other end ①. Do not try to twist both ropes together as this causes tension and the dough will split. Cut the rope to the length you want and wet the ends to hold it in place.

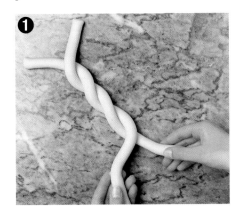

## MAKING A PLAITED ROPE
Start with three, evenly thick sausages of dough. Stick them together at one end with a little water and then lay the right-hand rope over the middle one to become the central rope ①. Do the same with the rope on the left, taking it over to the middle ②. Keeping the tension even as you work, repeat until you have the required length. A plaited rope looks equally pretty if it is worked in three different colours.

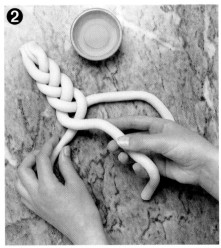

## MAKING UNCUT EDGES
In my early experiments with napkin rings, I rolled the dough into a flat sheet and then cut out strips of dough. However, a cut edge can look very untidy and so, to make neat edges for napkin rings and flat basket weave, for example, try this method.

Roll out a sausage of dough and use a rolling pin to flatten to the desired width and length ①. This results in an uncut edge that is far neater than cutting the dough with a knife. It is best to avoid using extra flour for rolling out if possible as it tends to dry the dough and cause the edges to crack.

## MAKING TEMPLATES
There are several ways of making templates. For a simple outline, either use the templates given at the back of this book (see pages 179-180) or draw your own on cardboard. To transfer the outlines on pages 179-180, trace over the appropriate shape using tracing paper and a pencil. Then draw over the outline on the back of the paper, position it on the cardboard and go over the top one more time. Cut out the resulting shape and use this by laying it on rolled out dough and cutting around the edge ①. Remember, though, that some of the most natural looking leaves are those that are cut freehand using a sharp, pointed knife.

Alternatively, draw around fresh leaves to make cardboard patterns ②. Or make your own, re-usable, patterns by drawing around or photocopying the leaves and then sticking the outline to some cardboard and cutting out ③.

## MAKING NAPKIN RINGS

Many of the ideas in this book can be adapted to make napkin rings which are a simple and attractive way to finish off a table setting. Before making the ring itself, cover a cardboard roll with aluminium foil and then roll out strips of dough, fold around the roll and stick the ends together with some water ①. Decorate as appropriate.

## MAKING FRUITS & BERRIES

Here is a selection of fruits to start you off but you will soon find you are experimenting with others. As there are many different ways of forming fruits, use the following instructions as a guide to get you started.

• **APPLES** Roll a ball to the required size. Push a blunted pencil into the top and insert a piece of twig for the stalk. If the bottom of the apple will be seen, mark the bottom by using a modelling tool. Finish with a clove ①. If you do not have a modelling tool, use a Phillips screwdriver, a drill countersinking bit or mark with a cocktail stick.

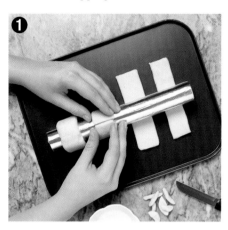

• **BANANAS** Take a piece of dough the same size as you would for an apple and roll to the required length. Use a knife to flatten the roll so that it has four or five sides and then elongate the top. Form the bottom of the banana and roughen the end using a cocktail stick ②. These bananas look best when made into bunches of three or five joined at the top.

• **BLACKBERRIES** Roll a ball about the size of a large pea and make a large number of tiny balls the size of a glass head pin. Wet the tiny balls and cover the surface of the berry. Add a calyx and stalk if you wish ③.

• **GRAPES** Make dozens of small balls of dough first and then pick them up in your hands, add a few drops of water to help them stick and then 'pour' them in place ④. If the grapes are to be left unpainted, carefully stick each one in place so that they do not stain during baking. Cut a leaf and scrunch it up on the top of the bunch. Finish off with a twig stalk ⑤.

• **KIWI FRUITS** Start with a ball of dough rolled into an oval. Wet the surface and then cover it with garlic-pressed dough cut off in minute lengths to give a woolly effect ⑥.

• **KUMQUATS** Make an oval ball to the required size and then roll it over the finest part of a cheese grater to give a realistic texture. Mark the bottom of each kumquat with a modelling tool and insert a wet clove ⑦.

• **LEMONS** These are formed from balls of dough which are rolled into shape and then textured all over with each lemon with a fine grater. A clove is pushed into one end ⑧.

• **LOGANBERRIES** Make as for blackberries, but start with a cone shape rather than the blackberry's ball. Cover the cone with the small balls, starting at the tip of the cone and working towards the wider end.
• **ORANGES** These are larger versions of a kumquat, but spherical. Make as for kumquats, above.

• **PEACHES** Make a ball from the same size piece as you would for an apple. Use the back of a knife to slightly indent one side. Make a smooth indentation for the top with a blunt pencil or modelling tool ⑨.

• **PEARS** These are also the same proportion as apples. Start by making a ball and then use one finger to roll one end thinner. Push a wet twig in the top and indent the bottom and finish off with a clove ⑩.

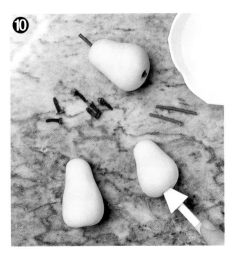

• **PLUMS** Take a piece of dough about half the size required for an apple. Roll to an oval. Use the back of a knife to indent one side ⑪.

• **POMEGRANATES** Make these from a ball of dough that is elongated at one end to form a crown. Push a pencil into the top to hollow it out and then snip carefully V-shapes out of this and fan out ⑫.

• **STRAWBERRIES** Make a small ball of dough and then roll into a cone shape using one finger. Take a cocktail stick (toothpick) and mark the pips by gently pressing it into the dough at an angle. Make a calyx by using a commercial cutter or use one of the calyx templates on page 180. Wet it and then press into place using a smooth modelling tool. This will make the tips of the calyx stand up and therefore quite fragile. Stick them down onto the berry if you prefer. Add a tiny stalk made from dough ⑬.

## MAKING VEGETABLES & SEEDS

There are far too many vegetables to show you all of them here, but these basic ones will give you a start. Try also making peppers, onions, parsnips, corn-on-the-cob and runner beans.

• **ACORNS** Take a small piece of dough and roll it into a ball and then elongate it to make an acorn. Next, take a slightly smaller piece of dough, roll into a ball and then cup in the palm of your hand using one finger. Wet the cup and mould it around the acorn ①. Use a cheese grater to make the suitable texture on the cup. Add a twig stalk ②.

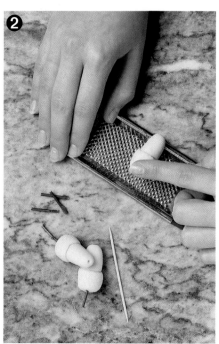

• **BRUSSELS SPROUTS** Start with a tiny ball of dough and build up layers of leaves on it by cutting out circles of dough using a 2 cm (¾ in) cutter or bottle top. Vein these either by imprinting with a real leaf or use a knife (see page 44) and apply to the ball overlapping each one slightly. Continue to the required size ③.

• **BUTTON MUSHROOMS** Take a small ball of dough and cup it in your hand using a finger. Roll out a length of dough for stalks if you are making several and cut into short pieces. Wet the cup and mould around the stalk ④.

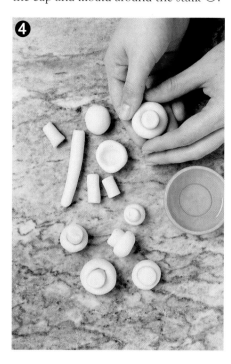

• **CARROTS** Roll a ball of dough into a conical shape and then make several small, shallow indentations around the carrot using the back of a knife ⑤. Indent the top, too. Then make carrot tops by rolling out a thin length of dough and cutting it up into five pieces of roughly equal length. Wet these and push into the top of the carrot ⑥.

• **CAULIFLOWER FLORETS** Start off with a small ball of dough and elongate part of it to make a short, stumpy stalk with a flattened end ⑦. Press the head into fine netting to give it some suitably cauliflower-like texture, and then use the back of a knife to mark stalks ⑧.

**7**

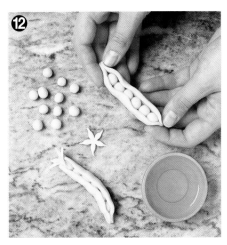

**12**

• **LEEKS** Leeks are made from several layers and so begin by making a central 6 mm (¼ in) sausage of dough about 2.5-5 cm (1-2 in) shorter than the finished leek. Roll out an oblong of dough thinly and wrap the central core in this ⑩. The next sheet should be slightly wider. Wrap the leek so that this time the seam is on the opposite side to the first. Repeat with as many layers as you wish. Fan out the top. Pinch in the bottom and make roots by pressing a small ball of dough through a garlic press. Cut off and attach ⑪.

• **SEED PODS** Roll out a ball of dough into an oval shape, wet the surface and fill with dozens of small balls to represent seeds. Close the pod up slightly and nip the ends together ⑬.

**8**

**10**

• **FIELD MUSHROOMS** Take a ball of dough and flatten onto your palm. This will make the dough domed on one side. Using a small sharp knife, mark the gills very closely together all the way around on the underside. Indent the centre of the mushroom, and make a stalk from a piece of rolled dough, pointed at one end ⑨.

**13**

• **TOMATOES** Make a ball. Cut out a calyx either freehand or using the calyx templates on page 180, wet the back of it and press onto the tomato with a pointed tool or blunt pencil. Add a dough stalk if you wish ⑭.

**9**

**11**

• **PEAPODS** Cut an oval of dough the length of the required pod. Form several small peas and place along the length of the pod. Damp the sides and pinch up around the peas. Add a small calyx and dough stalk ⑫.

**14**

## MAKING LEAVES & PETALS

You can spend as much as you like on commercial cutters and there are a huge number on the market for the cake icing trade. You will learn by trial and error how thick to make them so that they do not break. As a general rule, any leaf which overlaps a basket or garland and is unsupported should be 3-6 mm (⅛-¼ in) thick.

Basic leaves can be made using a circular cutter. If you don't have any, start collecting tins of various sizes ranging from tomato purée to tuna fish: they make excellent cutters, but make sure you use a tin opener that doesn't remove the top of the tin as the edges can then be dangerously sharp. For very small leaves, a bottle top is ideal.

First cut out the circle and then cut into it again to make a leaf shape ①. The length and width may be varied as much as you require at this stage.

For lilac leaves, start with a circle,

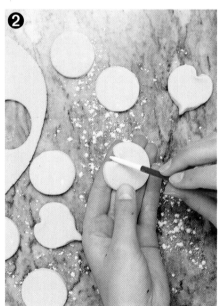

indent the top of each leaf with the end of a paintbrush ② and pinch the other end to make a point ③. Mark the leaf veins using the back of a knife ④, a commercial leaf veiner or, better still, a fresh leaf. When attaching the leaves to their base, give each one a slight twist as they then look far more natural. For variations in leaf shape see Making Templates on page 180.

• **MAKING ROSES** Roses are a very popular adornment for salt dough models. They can be made in various sizes and painted all sorts of colours — just like the real thing. Start by rolling a small cone of dough to form the centre of the flower. Then cut out several petals using either a cutter or one of the templates on page 180 (depending on how large you wish your

rose to be). Using water to keep the petals in place, first fold one around the central cone, and then another making sure that you overlap the first petal on both sides ⑤. Then take three petals, overlap them and fold around the central petals ⑥. Repeat with five petals in the same way, gently fanning out each one to make a gloriously full and blousy rose ⑦.

# BAKING DOUGH

It is important to bake your dough as soon as your model is complete to prevent the edges from drying out. This will ensure that your models are strong. However, as oven temperatures vary enormously, a certain am ount of experimenting is needed to find what works well in your oven. The general rule is not to hurry it. A sudden blast of hot air will cause trapped air to expand and spoil your work. On the other hand, too cool a drying process means that the chemical change needed to bond the ingredients does not take place and the model will be very fragile.

## FAN OVENS
As fan ovens cook faster and tend to be hotter than convection ovens, start cooking at 80 °C (175 °F). As a rule, I cook all my dough overnight and only the thinnest items are dry by morning. All items must be baked until solid. Test by trying to stick in a pin: it will be impossible once hard. Alternatively, turn your model over and check the back for dryness, pressing behind the thickest part. There should be no 'give' at all. If there is, remove the model from the baking tray, place it on a cooling rack and continue cooking.

If you wish to speed up the baking process after about 12 hours, gradually increase the temperature to 130 °C (250 °F) by raising the temperature 10 °C (25 °F) at a time every 20-30 minutes until the model is dry. Very large models will bake quickly at this temperature. Be warned though — the dough will darken with the increase in temperature but you can use this to your advantage should you want it to appear more golden ①. When dry, turn off the oven and leave your dough to cool down slowly.

## CONVECTION OVENS
Start cooking at 100 °C (210 °F) and continue until solid, or increase the temperature as above, adding 10-20 °C (25-50 °F) degrees to the temperatures.

## GAS OVENS
Gas has a high moisture content which is ideal for cooking salt dough as it

allows the inside to dry far more quickly. As a result, however, there is a higher risk of the dough rising or cracking early in the drying process. So the following method is recommended to prevent this from happening.

For the first hour, cook at Gas mark ¼ with the door open. Prick any air bubbles which appear during this time with a pin. For the next hour, leave the door half open, and finally close it and continue cooking until the model is thoroughly dried. Make sure that any young children (and pets!) are well out of the way if using a gas oven with the door open.

## MICROWAVES
This is a wonderful way of cooking salt dough and achieving very quick results although it is more likely to bubble up than with conventional cooking so it needs careful monitoring. It is particularly good when making dough with impatient children who want to see instant results.

Place the dough models — remember not to add anything metallic to your design if you are going to cook it in this way — on a plate (no grease required). Set the oven on defrost or the lowest setting and cook for five minutes at a time. Between cooking sessions, open

the door to allow any steam to escape; leave for a few minutes and repeat. When the model is almost dry, reduce the length of cooking time and monitor progress very carefully. As with everything cooked in the microwave, experimentation is necessary and the cooking times will vary depending on the weight of dough being cooked. A small piece of jewellery, for example, will take up to 20 minutes to cook in this way.

## AIR DRYING
I have made several attempts to air dry dough but have found that the models dried in this way are extremely fragile and so I would only recommend it for repairing broken, varnished dough. Remake the broken part and then lay the dough in a warm, dry place where the air can circulate, until the dough has hardened.

---

### HINTS AND TIPS

- Once the model is really firm and comes off the baking tray easily, put it on a cooling tray and return it to the oven to allow it to continue drying underneath.

- A project that takes a long time to cook can be somewhat inconvenient. A solid fuel cooker is the solution — if not yours, then a friend's perhaps. Start off cooking in the bottom of the coolest oven for about 12 hours, remove from the tray to a rack and move up to the next oven and continue until dry.

- Leave models in the oven until cold or remove and place on a cooling tray if the oven is still in use or you are using a solid fuel stove.

- If you are not planning on painting or varnishing immediately, store in a tin to prevent absorption of moisture.

---

### SAFETY NOTE
Never rebake a repaired varnished model as the fumes given off may be toxic and flammable.

# PAINTING

This is the one thing that gives many students a problem. I include myself in this as I found it very difficult to get over the 'I can't paint' barrier. Well, you can with practice. The best way to start is to make a few extra leaves, fruits, vegetables, and so on, and bake these alongside your masterpieces. Practise painting on the spare leaves and fruits, and once you feel you are good enough, progress to your models. Decide what effect you want from your painting. You may decide to paint with solid colour for a simple rustic effect or you may prefer to build up the colour for a more natural appearance.

## WHICH PAINTS?

There are a number of paints on the market which can be used for salt dough, but why not start by using paints you may already have? Water colours give a lovely translucent and rustic appearance, and poster paints may also be used for a slightly denser effect. For leaves, try using a light wash of sap green and the add a little brown to darken the centre of the leaf. For blossoms use a pale colour on the edge and deeper in the centre ①. Apples look particularly good if first painted with a wash of yellow ochre. Then dry brush a little orange on one side and finish with some alizarin crimson to give a stripy effect. Alizarin crimson and black mixed together look very good on blackberries ②.

• **GOUACHE PAINTS** Gouache is a dense form of water colour and these are very useful for getting a solid covering. I like to use red gouache for painting strawberries and holly berries and they can be very effective used in conjunction with any other water-based paints. The density of gouache paints can be very useful. For example, my first attempt at painting the cat on page 35 was to make him a tabby cat, but as my painting was so bad I decided to change him to a smart black cat ③.

• **ACRYLIC HOBBY PAINTS** These come in a wide variety of colours and are very fast drying. As they are made with a base of PVA glue, make sure that brushes are washed out carefully immediately after use as they cannot be salvaged once dry. Remove any splashes from clothing straight away.

• **ENAMEL PAINTS** Enamel paints are an expensive alternative and unsuitable for children to use as they are difficult to remove from clothing. They are also solvent-based so use in a well-ventilated room. Brushes must be cleaned using thinners. Aerosol varnish should be used as the solvent in varnish will cause the colours to run if you are using a brush.

• **GOLD AND SILVER PAINTS** As long as they are either gouache or acrylic paints, gold and silver can be used before baking, but enamel should be used afterwards. Enamel gold and silver gives a really bright finish, but gold and silver poster paints tend to be affected by the salt, and turn green! I recently tried to add glitter to some dough Christmas decorations before baking, with the same result. So add glue and glitter after varnishing.

# VARNISHING

Before varnishing, allow models to dry for 24 hours — or speed up the process with a hair dryer on its lowest setting. Due to the high salt content in the dough, it will quickly absorb moisture if not sealed. This is done by using at least two coats of clear polyurethane varnish or lacquer. As there are a large number of varnishes on the market, it is best to try two or three to get the effect you want. Generally speaking, if the varnish is High Build, or feels thick when shaken, you will need to apply fewer coats than some other makes. You may find that the varnish darkens and thickens near the end of the tin and in this case, keep it for varnishing the backs of your models and buy fresh varnish for the fronts. Both matt and gloss varnish may be used to seal the dough and may even be used on the same item. For example, you may wish to use matt for a tree trunk and gloss for the leaves.

Varnish the back first by placing your model upside down on a pillow to prevent damage to any delicate surface decoration. Protect the pillow by covering it with an old sheet of unprinted plastic (the inside of a carrier bag is ideal) or silicone paper. Leave to dry for about four hours between coats and at least 12 hours before varnishing the front. Check that varnish has not run through and spoilt the front between coats.

Clean the brush with white spirit between varnishes and when you have finished varnishing, wipe the brush on a paper towel and then clean thoroughly in white spirit.

• Tip: Buy your own brush. No one can then blame you for letting it go crusty!

## HANGING DOUGH MODELS

There are various ways of hanging dough models. On small pieces, a bent piece of stub wire may be pushed into the model while it is still damp. Alternatively, use a hair pin or a paper clip, both of which are coated and will not rust. If you prefer to hang with ribbon, make a hole in the dough using a drinking straw to remove a neat core.

On larger items it is best to think about hanging once they are dry. Fixing wire in the back is the best as a good hanging angle can be achieved, it is strong and also invisible. Turn the model over and support on a pillow. Using a very fine drill, make two holes in which to glue wire with either two-part epoxy resin or hot glue. On really large items, glue screw-in eyes in place

and connect with picture wire for maximum support. Door name plates may be held in place with double-sided sticky pads.

The most important thing to tell any recipient of your dough is to hang it in a dry atmosphere and it will last indefinitely. The danger time for dough is late autumn and winter when unheated porches, cloakrooms and hallways are subject to becoming damp.

⚠️
### SAFETY NOTE
Never hang salt dough above a bed or within reach of a child's cot in case it should break unexpectedly. This can happen very occasionally for no apparent reason. Neither should you give dough items to young children to play with — and always make sure that any model that looks good enough to eat is well out of their reach.

## TROUBLESHOOTING

• **BREAKAGES** These happen with frustrating frequency, particularly when you first start! Overhanging leaves are especially vulnerable but it is possible to salvage them using a solvent glue or, better still, a two-part epoxy resin or hot glue for an even stronger bond. Be very careful to wipe away any excess glue on the surface as water soluble paints will not cover it.

Alternatively, it is sometimes better to paint the model and any broken pieces first, then glue later. Badly broken parts may be reformed with fresh dough and left to air dry (see page 45), or be re-baked if the dough has not been varnished. This method is surprisingly successful.

• **BUBBLING** Many a work of art has been spoilt by being baked too quickly causing trapped air to rise. Poor or insufficient kneading can also be to blame. Try to make flat areas with fresh, unused dough and roll it out just once if possible. Flour, used for rolling, can get trapped in the dough in layers and cause a puff pastry effect. So if you have to start again, re-knead the dough very thoroughly.

• **CRACKS** Cracks may appear at any time during baking or during the following hours or weeks, and large, flat areas of dough seem to be the most vulnerable. Always use the minimum quantity of water to get a workable dough and avoid stretching it when transferring to the baking tray.

If cracks do appear, allow them to fully develop for several days before repairing with softened fresh dough and re-baking. If you are planning a dense coat of paint, ready-made plaster filler is a really good way of mending cracks and it sets hard within hours. The filler can then be sanded to give it a good, neat finish.

• **DOUGH BECOMES SOFT** This is due to the high salt content which allows the dough to absorb moisture from the atmosphere. If a model should become soft, place it in an airing cupboard or above a radiator until it hardens again and then revarnish and hang in a dry place.

# LEMON-EDGED BOWL

*Just the thing to fill with fruits or a selection of nuts, this bowl was made as part of a set which includes napkin rings, a candle holder and twisted garland. The little flowers appear blue next the yellow but were painted with a mixture of Payne's grey and white.*

1 Roll two-thirds of the dough on a lightly floured work surface to a thickness of 6 mm (¼ in). Carefully lift up the dough with the rolling pin and place it carefully into the dish, avoiding stretching which could cause the dough to split during cooking.

## YOU WILL NEED

| |
|---|
| 1 batch of dough (page 36) |
| Rolling pin |
| Pie dish with rim, 21 cm (8½ in) diameter, lightly greased |
| Knife |
| Container of water |
| Leaf cutter or template (page 180) |
| Fine grater |
| Cloves |
| Blossom cutter or template (page 180) |
| Paints (page 46) |
| Paintbrushes |
| Varnish (pages 46-47) |

## VARIATIONS

Edge your bowl with oranges, strawberries, apples — indeed use any fruit, vegetable or flower that you care to make. If you prefer a latticework basket, line the dish with woven strips of dough (see page 38) or use a lattice pie cutter.

**2** Trim the dough about 6 mm (¼ in) in from the edge of the dish and flatten all around. To neaten the edge, roll two sausages of dough 7 mm (⁵⁄₁₆ in) thick and form a twisted rope (see page 39) that is long enough to fit half way around the dish. Repeat for the other side. It is easier to make the rope in two pieces than trying to fit one length all the way around.

**3** Cut out leaves using the cutter or template. Mark the veins and lay the leaves in place making sure that the joins in the rope are covered. Form lemons from elongated balls of dough (see page 41), push a clove in one end of each and place the lemons around the edge of the bowl over the groups of leaves.

**4** Add a few blossoms using the blossom cutter or template. Fasten them in place with a drop of water, grouping them on the leaves and near the lemons. If you are using the cutter, stick each blossom in place as you cut them out; for blossoms cut from a template it is far easier to cut out a batch at a time.

**5** Bake immediately at about 80 °C (175 °F) (fan oven) or 100 °C (210 °F) (convection oven) for 12-18 hours, or gas mark ¼ for 6-9 hours, or until solid (see page 45). Keep checking for any bubbles forming on the base during the first hour of cooking. If they appear, prick them with a pin. Then paint and varnish the bowl if you wish (see page 46) or leave the dough natural. I painted the bowl with magnolia emulsion and then used sap green mixed with a little brown for the leaves, Payne's grey and white for the flowers, and cadmium yellow for the lemons.

# GRAPES TRINKET DISH

*Here is a good way of using small amounts of dough which would make a very acceptable present. There are three different versions to choose from, and they are each easy to make. Why not make the matching earrings and brooch and give them to a friend?*

**1** Roll the dough on a lightly floured work surface to a thickness of 6 mm (¼ in). Carefully lift up the dough with the rolling pin and place it into the bowl, avoiding stretching which could cause the dough to split during cooking. Either form a twisted rope edge from 6 mm (¼ in) thick sausages of dough (see page 39) or make ivy leaves using the cutter or template and place them around the edge.

## YOU WILL NEED

Small amount of dough (page 36)

Rolling pin

Round dish, 9.5 cm (3½ in) long, lightly greased

Container of water

Ivy leaf cutter or template (page 180)

A few twigs

Greaseproof paper

Paints (page 46)

Paintbrushes

Varnish (pages 46-47)

Jewellery findings

Two-part epoxy resin or hot glue

### — VARIATIONS —

See the gift ideas gallery on pages 66-67 for other jewellery ideas and design dishes to match.

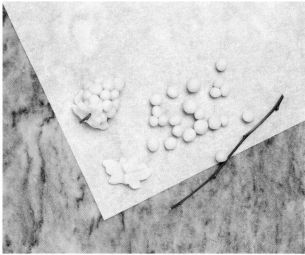

2 Make the grapes from dozens of tiny balls of dough. Add a few drops of water to them in your hand and carefully 'pour' them in place, avoiding getting any water on the dish which will stain during cooking. Add grape leaves, making them with the cutter or template, and a twig stalk.

3 Make the earrings by cutting out two leaves for each one and place them on greaseproof paper, overlapping in opposite directions. Make lots of small grapes and pile them on top of the leaves using water, as described in Step 2. It is a good idea to make spares at this stage as they are quick to make and fairly fragile. The brooch was formed by starting with a sausage of dough which the leaves were placed on.

4 Bake immediately at about 80 °C (175 °F) (fan oven) or 100 °C (210 °F) (convection oven) for 4-6 hours, or gas mark ¼ for 2-3 hours, or until solid (see page 45). Then paint (see page 46). I painted the leaves with a light wash of sap green tinged with brown, and the grapes are brilliant violet mixed with Payne's grey.

5 Once the paint has dried, glue the appropriate findings onto the back of the pieces of jewellery using the two-part epoxy resin or hot glue. Metal does not stick well to varnish so glue on the findings prior to varnishing. When varnishing, take care that you don't get a pool in the bottom of the trinket dish.

# BASKETS AND BOWLS GALLERY

### Woven wheat-edged basket

Strips of dough have been woven together and baked in a glass pie dish. A potato ricer was then used for the wheat stalks and the ears of wheat snipped using scissors.

### Cluster of fruits-edged bowl

Made with a lattice pie cutter, the twisted rope then encircles three-quarters of the edge and the leaves and flowers — highlighted with watercolours — nestle in the gap.

### Natural dough, nut and fir cone dish

A twisted rope curls around the top of this dish (made with a pie cutter) decorated with fir cones, nuts and dough fruits. This is a good one to start with as it is quick to make.

### Greek key bowl

To make the regular key pattern around the edge of this bowl, I pressed a length of shiny cord into the dough. To finish it off, the top is made from a simply twisted rope.

### Dough fruits cooked in a wicker basket

This basket has been lined with a dough cloth, filled with scrunched-up foil, and then covered with dough fruits. Make sure you use a wicker basket which has not been varnished as it will fume when cooking.

### Star-edged dish

Stars and holly leaves were attached to the edge of this simply made bowl. Unfortunately, water got on the base during this process so it is not too beautiful — hence the doily. The stars are painted with a lovely gold gouache.

# PRIMROSE AND APPLE BLOSSOM GARLAND

*Capture spring with this delicate coloured swag of trailing ivy and flowers. It would look very pretty hanging above a dresser or sideboard. If you do not have a large enough baking tray for this project, make it up in three pieces and stick them together before painting.*

**1** Roll out half the dough into a thick sausage about 84 cm (33 in) long. Roll it slightly to flatten to 4 cm (1½ in) wide and then place on the baking tray. Cut out the primrose and apple leaves either by cutting around a few different sized fresh ones or use the templates on page 180. Vein the leaves (see page 44) and place them on the garland overlapping the edges. Make plenty so that the garland is nearly covered at this stage.

## — VARIATIONS —

Why not make a matching trinket dish for a dresser? Holly and Christmas roses would make a very festive variation.

**2** Cut out apple blossoms using the 2.5 cm (1 in) blossom cutter or template, and press in place with the pointed tool or pencil. Similarly, cut out primroses using the cutter or template, and press into position with the star pointed tool.

**3** To make apple blossom buds, use the small blossom cutter to make the calyx and mould it over a pea-sized ball of dough. Make plenty of these and place in little clusters along the garland. Thinly roll sausages of dough for the trailing ivy and then cut out three sizes of ivy leaf graduating the sizes from large to small.

**4** To form rosettes, roll a sausage of dough to 25 cm (10 in) long and flatten to 4 cm (1½ in) wide. Wet along one edge, pleat into a circle and attach to the top left corner of the garland. Repeat for the top right corner of the garland.

**5** Bake immediately at about 80 °C (175 °F) (fan oven) or 100 °C (210 °F) (convection oven) for 18-24 hours, or gas mark ¼ for 9-12 hours, or until solid (see page 45). Then paint and varnish (see pages 46-47). I painted the apple blossom with permanent rose gouache paint tinged with white towards the edges, the leaves are sap green, the ivy Hooker's green, and the primroses are cadmium yellow with a touch of yellow ochre in their centres. Drill and glue in wires on both sides for hanging (see page 47).

# TWISTED AUTUMN GARLAND

*Why not capture an autumn walk on this colourful garland? Hunt for beech nut shells and real acorns, or make dough acorns as I have. Substitute little fir cones for the nuts if you wish. This garland would look equally good if left unpainted.*

**1** Take two-thirds of the dough and roll into two long, thick sausages. Lay one sausage over the other, twist into a rope (see page 39) and then make into a circle with a diameter of 23 cm (9 in) on the baking tray. Make the join at the bottom where it will not be seen. Finally, flatten 10 cm (4 in) along the bottom.

## YOU WILL NEED

| |
|---|
| 1 batch of dough (page 36) |
| Rolling pin |
| Baking tray, lightly greased |
| Container of water |
| Sharp knife |
| Leaf cutter or template (page 180) |
| Pointed modelling tool or old pencil |
| A few twigs |
| Beech nuts |
| Hazel nuts |
| Almonds |
| Acorn leaf cutter or template (page 180) |
| Drinking straw |
| Ribbon or drill, glue and wire for hanging |
| Paints (page 46) |
| Paintbrushes |
| Varnish (pages 46-47) |

## VARIATIONS

This garland can be adapted for any season. Make lilac for early summer, or masses of roses and sprigs of lavender. For Easter, how about primroses and little decorated eggs? Holly, Christmas roses, fir cones and tangerines tied with a rich red satin ribbon would make a perfect present.

2 Cut some leaves either freehand or using the leaf cutter or template. Fix in place along the bottom of the ring and then make three apples (see page 40) and position on top of the leaves. Make five blackberries (see page 40) and four or five acorns (see page 42) and also push into position.

3 Fill gaps with beech nut shells, hazel nuts and almonds. Then add a few small oak leaves using the cutter or template to make them before positioning over the nuts.

4 If you want to hang the garland with ribbon, core out two holes with the drinking straw. If you prefer to hang it invisibly, drill and add wire after the wreath has been baked.

5 Bake immediately at about 80 °C (175 °F) (fan oven) or 100 °C (210 °F) (convection oven) for 18-24 hours, or gas mark ¼ for 9-12 hours, or until solid (see page 45). Then paint and varnish (see pages 46-47). I painted the leaves with sap green tinged with brown, the blackberries are a mixture of alizarin crimson and Payne's grey, and the apples ochre and orange, finished off with a dry brush of alizarin crimson.

# GARLANDS AND WREATHS GALLERY

### Natural dough garland
This was made from a small quantity of left-over dough and decorated with seedpods and tiny cones.

### Buckwheat, rye and plain flour wreath
These delightful mice nestling in their flowerpots were made from a mixture of doughs and the pots were half filled with aluminium foil to speed the baking process.

## Fruited swag

This magnificent wall hanging was
made using three batches of
dough. The base is covered
with leaves, fruit and
flowers so that none of
it shows through.

## Ribbons and cherries

This colourful garland was quickly made
from about half a batch of dough.

# SHELL MIRROR

*This Shaker-style frame will look good in any warm, dry bathroom. I have made it from a mixture of shells, some found on a shell beach on holiday, and some purchased. I fell in love with the glass nuggets and just had to include them. Look out for green or blue nuggets which might look even better. The mirror can be hung using rope or sisal, or drill and stick on a wire hook if you prefer.*

**1** Make a cardboard template 20.5 cm (8¼ in) square with an aperture of 9 cm (3½ in). Roll some of the dough to a thickness of 8 mm (⅜ in). Mark the hanging holes 2.5 cm (1 in) in from the edges using the cocktail stick (toothpick). Lay the template over the rolled dough and cut around the frame and aperture with the craft knife. Smooth the edges and core out the hanging holes using the drinking straw.

## YOU WILL NEED

Cardboard

Scissors

1 batch of dough (page 36)

Rolling pin

Baking tray, lightly greased

Craft knife

Cocktail stick (toothpick)

Pencil

Large drinking straw

Container of water

Garlic press

Seaweed templates (page 180)

Knife

Shells

Glass nuggets

Craft glue

Varnish (pages 46-47)

Paintbrush

Mirror

Silicone sealant

Felt and card for backing (optional)

Sisal rope or raffia for hanging

2 Use the garlic press to form seaweed arranged in little clumps around the frame, and then cut some larger pieces of seaweed fronds either freehand or using the template.

3 Press shells into the dough, scattering them around the frame. Also add little clusters of nuggets in either one, or a selection of colours.

4 Bake immediately at about 80 °C (175 °F) (fan oven) or 100 °C (210 °F) (convection oven) for 8-12 hours, or at Gas mark ¼ for 4-6 hours, or until solid (see page 45). The glass nuggets will stubbornly refuse to stick to the dough once it is cooked, so they will need to be stuck in place with craft glue at this stage. Paint if you wish, and then varnish (see pages 46-47). I used some Hooker's green and then a wash of gold gouache on the shells. If you use matt varnish, you may prefer not to get any on the nuggets as it dulls them.

5 Glue the mirror to the back of the frame using silicone sealant, or some other suitable glue, and cover if you wish with felt-covered card. Thread sisal, rope or raffia through the hanging holes and adjust to the required length.

## VARIATIONS

Why not tie up bundles of soaps with matching rope or raffia decorated with shells? Likewise, glass jars filled with shells and pebbles always look pretty. If you use shells you have collected, why not put a holiday snapshot in the frame instead of the mirror?

# MIRRORS AND FRAMES GALLERY

## *Seashore walk mirror*

This pretty frame is made of a collection of driftwood, glass, shells, dried seaweed and stones. The mermaid, rusty anchor, and treasure chest add a little fantasy.

## Grape and fig mirror

This mirror started life as a disaster as it was an early effort at framing a mirror and the dough broke in two during baking. I salvaged it and think that the silver gouache added to the paints gives a lustrous finish.

## Heart frame

I used a large heart-shaped cutter to make this frame which would be delightful scaled down as a tree decoration.

## Trellis frame

Wild strawberries and ivy combine to make this frame. The outline was drawn on silicone paper and the dough cut to size.

# TEDDY BEAR BOOK ENDS

*The weight of salt dough makes it ideal for these delightful book ends. Make the supports from an extra batch of dough if you are not able to make the wooden bases and allow plenty of time for baking. This project requires some patience but it will be well rewarded. They could be personalized for a child by writing the titles of their favourite stories on the covers of the books. The possibilities are endless!*

**1** Start by making the bookends. Sand the edges of the wood, round off the corners and then glue the shorter piece of wood to the longer pieces. Hammer in two panel pins for extra strength and once the glue is dry, carefully fill the nail holes with filler. Finish off with the varnish or the coloured satin wood stain.

## YOU WILL NEED

| |
|---|
| 2 pieces of wood 13 x 9 cm (5¼ x 3½ in) |
| 2 pieces of wood 14.5 x 9 cm (5¾ x 3½ in) |
| Sandpaper |
| Wood glue |
| Hammer |
| 4 panel pins |
| Wood filler |
| Varnish or satin wood stain |
| **For the teddies** |
| 1 batch of dough (page 36) |
| Rolling pin |
| Knife |
| Container of water |
| Peppercorns |
| Cocktail stick (toothpick) |
| Deep square or oblong cake tin, lined and lightly greased |
| Paints (page 46) |
| Paintbrushes |
| Varnish (pages 46-47) |
| Craft glue |

### VARIATIONS

Let your imagination run wild — how about replacing the teddies with keep-fit pigs, sleeping cats, or sheep sitting knitting.

**2** Now make the teddies by forming a body shape with indentations for the legs and arms. Make the arms by rolling enough dough for four and cutting into four equal sized pieces for both teddies. This helps to ensure all the arms are the same size. Repeat for the legs, turning up the ends to make feet.

**3** Make the heads from balls of dough. Make indentations for the eyes and press in peppercorns. Mark noses and mouths using the knife and stick on their ears. Texturize the teddies with the cocktail stick — it will feel like it takes forever (see page 38 for alternative methods of adding texture).

**4** Piece together the teddies on the lined and lightly greased cake tin and then make their accessories. Make a stack of little books and one open book from thinly rolled dough, marking the pages with a knife. Give one teddy a bow tie cut from rolled dough. Make a hot water bottle and mark it with a criss-cross pattern.

**5** Bake immediately at a 45-degree angle to preserve the shapes. One of my bears sagged a little in the oven but it has given him extra character. He looks very relaxed! Bake at about 80 °C (175 °F) (fan oven) or 100 °C (210 °F) (convection oven) for 18-24 hours, or at Gas mark ¼ for 9-12 hours, or until solid (see page 45). Then paint and varnish (see pages 46-47). I used a light wash of Vandyke brown for the bears and primary colours for the books. Finally, glue the teddies and books into place using a craft glue.

**⚠**
SAFETY NOTE
Remember that this is not a toy and is not suitable to be given to very young children.

# GIFT IDEAS GALLERY

## Napkin rings

These are easy to make to match candle holders or centrepieces.

## Paperweights

Unless you particularly want an extremely heavy paperweight, make it with a small ball of aluminium foil in the centre to allow it to bake more quickly. Stick a piece of felt on the bottom to protect furniture.

## Badges and earrings

Badges, brooches and earrings can be made in almost any design but remember to make a left and right design for each pair of earrings.

## Gift tag and decoration ideas

Make your own gift tags from scraps of leftover dough. Make a tiny hole for threading ribbon through before you bake them and paint or write your message on the dough before varnishing.

## Light or blind pull

Take a piece of cord long enough for your project, tie a bead or button to the end of it and work the dough around it. Then suspend in the oven and bake at a very low temperature so that the cord does not melt.

## Pig in a parachute lampshade

This pig weighs a ton — to lighten the load incorporate a ball of foil in his tummy.

## Dominoes

Peppercorns were used instead of paint to mark the dots on these dominoes. Alternatively, indent the numbers with a flat-headed nail dipped in paint: it will save on painting later.

# TREE DECORATIONS

*There are many decorations that you can make for your tree but I have chosen just a few to give detailed instructions for making them. Start well before Christmas because the painting and varnishing are quite time-consuming and there are far too many other things to be thinking of at Christmas. Alternatively, have a Scandinavian theme for your tree and either leave the dough its natural colour or use coloured dough. The choice is yours.*

## CANDY CANE

This is a very simple and effective decoration to make. To save a lot of time, use coloured dough instead of painting when finished.

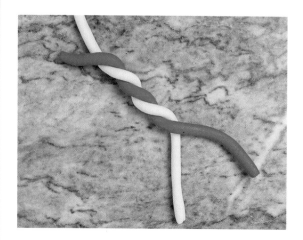

**1** Roll a small quantity of dough into a thin, even sausage about 15 cm (6 in) long and do the same with a little red dough. Then form the two pieces of dough into a twisted rope.

**2** Push a paper clip or wire hook into the top of the cane — unless you intend to hang it directly over the branch of the tree. Cut out three holly leaves from green dough and roll a few red berries. Use them to cover the hook. Finally, bake immediately at about 80 °C (175 °F) (fan oven) or 100 °C (210 °F) (convection oven) for 6-8 hours, or at Gas mark ¼ for 3-4 hours, or until solid, and then varnish.

1 batch of dough (page 36)

Red and green coloured doughs (optional)

Rolling pin

Baking trays, lightly greased

Paper clips or florist's stub wire

Ruler

Knife

Holly cutter or template (page 180)

Container of water

Garlic press

Pointed tool or pencil

Peppercorns

Large heart cutter or template (page 180)

Leaf cutter or template (page 180)

Briar rose cutter or template (page 180)

Pointed tool

Small heart cutter or template (page 180)

Star cutter or template (page 180)

Troll templates (page 179)

Paints (page 46)

Paintbrushes

Varnish (pages 46-47)

Pliers and wire cutters

# CHRISTMAS SHEEP

**1** Roll a little dough into sausages to make two legs, each about 5 cm (2 in) long and mark the hooves with the back of a knife. Make the body from an oval blob of dough and place on top of a baking tray.

**2** Now for the fun! Using the garlic press, push out 2.5 cm (1 in) lengths of dough and use this to cover the body starting from the outside and working in.

**3** Make a head from a small ball of dough and indent the eye sockets using the pointed tool or pencil. Push in wet peppercorns. Form tiny ears from squashed, rolled dough, folded at one end and then placed behind the head. Add horns too if you want.

**4** Cut out holly and roll berries from coloured dough and put in place. Push a piece of wire or a paper clip in for hanging. Then bake immediately at about 80 °C (175 °F) (fan oven) or 100 °C (210 °F) (convection oven) for 8-12 hours, or at Gas mark ¼ for 4-6 hours, or until solid, and then varnish.

## HEART-SHAPED DECORATIONS

These are quick to make using biscuit cutters or a template (see page 180).

**1** Roll out the dough to 6 mm (¼ in) thick and cut out heart shapes using the large cutter or template. Place onto a baking tray. Either make a little hole in the top for hanging, or push in a piece of wire or paper clip.

**2** Cut and vein leaves (see page 44) and lay in place. Add Christmas roses by cutting out five petals with the briar rose cutter or template and overlap them to make a circle. Push into position using the pointed tool.

**3** Finally, fill the centres with a few strands of garlic-pressed dough formed into a point. Bake immediately at 80 °C (175 °F) (fan oven) or 100 °C (210 °F) (convection oven) for 6-8 hours or at Gas mark ¼ for 3-4 hours, or until solid. Then paint and varnish (see pages 46-47). I painted the stamens and around the edge of the heart with a little gold gouache and the leaves are painted with diluted sap green mixed with brown.

## TWISTED GARLANDS WITH HANGING STAR OR HEART

These charming little garlands are simpler to make than they look!

**1** Make a twisted rope with either plain or coloured dough, or both, and join into a circle about 7.5 cm (3 in) in diameter. Lay on a baking tray. Push a 5 cm (2 in) length of wire through the top of the garland and cover the join with holly and berries made from coloured dough. Cut out a small heart or star shape using the cutters or templates and push a 2.5 cm (1 in) length of wire into it.

**2** Bake immediately at about 80 °C (175 °F) (fan oven) or 100 °C (210 °F) (convection oven) for 6-8 hours, or at Gas mark ¼ for 3-4 hours, or until solid (see page 45). Then paint and varnish (see pages 46-47). If you haven't used coloured dough, paint the heart with red gouache paint for a dense colour and the star with gold. Using pliers and wire cutters link the holly and berries to the dough, and then the heart or star. Bend and cut the wires to the correct length so that the heart or star hangs centrally in the garland.

# SCANDINAVIAN TROLL IN A STOCKING

This christmas decoration has been made with natural dough and painted with gouache paints after baking.

**1** Make a cone-shaped body with a small amount of dough (use the template on page 179 as a guide for the body's proportions) and make indentations for the arms and head. Make the troll's head from a ball of dough and add a tiny ball for her nose. Add eyes by making indents with the pointed tool and then roll a sausage of dough for her arms, cut in half at an angle and lay in place.

**3** Make the frill also from the template, then for the fur edging, cut some very short pieces of garlic-pressed dough and position the fur carefully right along the top of the stocking.

**2** Insert peppercorns into the eye sockets. Using the template, cut out a little dress from dough rolled to a thickness of 6 mm (¼ in) and stick in place. Repeat with the stocking shape.

**4** Again using the garlic press, make some long hair and curl it slightly as you position it. Cut out her hat using the template on page 179 and put in place. Now either push in a wire for hanging or drill and glue one in place later (see page 47). Bake immediately at 80 °C (175 °F) (fan oven) or 100 °C (210 °F) (convection oven) for 8-12 hours or at Gas mark ¼ for 4-6 hours, or until solid (see page 45). Then paint and varnish (see pages 46-47). I painted the troll with rich Mars red gouache. The gold stars were also painted with gouache. Vandyke brown was used for her hair and a very pale wash of yellow ochre for her face. Her cheeks were given a gentle pink tint.

# CHRISTMAS CANDLE HOLDER

*There is something really special about candlelight at Christmas and these candle holders are very simple to make. They can be decorated to coordinate with your table linen, or to fit in with any other celebration such as Thanksgiving or Easter. Make matching napkin rings too.*

**1** Roll some dough to a thickness of 6 mm (¼ in) and cut out a circle of 12 cm (4½ in) diameter. Place on the lightly greased baking tray. Cut a second circle 10-15 mm (½-¾ in) larger than the diameter of your candle and lay it either in the centre of the larger circle or slightly off-centre depending on your choice of design. Push the candle into the smaller circle of dough and mould the edges up around the candle. As the dough contracts during baking, move the candle around slightly to make the hole larger. Remove the candle.

2 Using the leaf cutter or template prepare as many leaves as are needed to cover the base (about 20). Vein them (see page 44) and position all over the base varying their angles and pinching some slightly to make the leaves look as realistic as possible.

3 Make poinsettias by cutting out ten petals for each flower, or use the calyx cutter or template. Cut out two sets for each flower and then position one on top of the other. Make the centres of each flower from a small cluster of tiny balls of dough, or one small ball textured with the cocktail stick (toothpick). Then add some Christmas roses (see page 70).

4 Bake immediately at about 80 °C (175 °F) (fan oven) or 100 °C (210 °F) (convection oven) for 8-12 hours, or at Gas mark ¼ for 4-6 hours, or until solid (see page 45). Then paint and varnish (see pages 46-47). I painted the leaves with Hooker's green tinged with brown, the poinsettias with alizarin crimson for the petals and cadmium yellow in the centres, and gold gouache for the rose centres.

5 Glue a circle of felt on the bottom to protect furniture. When the candle is lit, don't allow it to burn too low, and never leave it unattended.

### VARIATIONS

Use any of the ideas from this book to create your unique candle holder designs. Why not make a mass of tiny star-shaped candle holders for a really stunning display?

# FESTIVE DECORATIONS GALLERY

### Golden garland of Christmas fruits, holly and grapes

The perfect decoration to welcome your guests — as long as it is not hung outside.

### Holly brooch and earrings

This simple jewellery is very quick and easy to make and would sell well at a Christmas bazaar.

### Scandinavian trolls

These decorations are modelled in much the same way as the one on page 71.

### Christmas pudding fridge magnet

This magnet would be an ideal stocking filler, or it could be scaled down and used as jewellery.

## Snowman

This smiling fellow would be just as happy as a brooch or tree decoration instead of a fridge magnet.

## Goose plaque

A holiday in America was the inspiration for this snow goose. I first made a cardboard template and the goose was cut from 6 mm (¼ in) thick dough. The holly and berries were added at the end.

## Christmas bowl

What could be nicer than receiving this bowl filled with home-made Christmas biscuits or truffles and tied up in cellophane?

# DECOUPAGE

If you wish to take up a new craft, what could be easier than decoupage, as it really can be done anywhere? All you need are fine-pointed scissors — nail scissors will do the job very well — and PVA glue, which works both as an adhesive and as a varnish. Decoupage is one of those crafts which can be done in stages. So, if you want to, you can cut out motifs while watching the television or listening to the radio. The motifs can come from old magazines, greetings cards, wrapping paper, stamps, and jar labels, or you can cut or tear coloured paper into any shape you fancy. Once the motifs are ready, you will then only need a surface on which to decoupage which can be something as mundane as a shoe box or old sweet tin, or indeed any other container found about the house. Unlike painting, you don't need to be skilful, just careful.

With decoupage, you can achieve very sophisticated results from humble materials. In this book, for example, I have stuck motifs onto the inside of glass containers and then covered the whole interior with a coat of emulsion paint for a lovely translucent finish (see pages 84-85).

Or, by cutting out cat silhouettes from black sugar paper, I have transformed a plain white lampshade into a sophisticated shade fit for any cat lover (see pages 92-93). Both of these projects were incredibly quick to prepare and finish — just what is needed for a weekend's craft activity.

Decoupage is a great way of renewing items that look old, tired or scruffy. Among these pages you will find picture frames, candlesticks, a galvanized watering can, a toy box and a window box — look around your home and almost anything you set your eyes on can be covered in decoupage in one way or another. Even walls and doors can be decorated with this technique. Look in boot fairs and thrift shops for other items to decoupage such as chairs, tables, cupboards small and large, old wooden boxes and mirror frames.

Once you start working with decoupage, you may well find that it is one of those crafts that you won't want to stop. Also, because its essential materials such as emulsion or acrylic paints and PVA glue dry so quickly, decoupage really is the ideal weekend craft.

*Juliet Bawden*

# GETTING STARTED

*Decoupage is the art of decorating a surface with scraps or cutouts of printed images. It is a very straightforward process: select an image which is then carefully cut out, glue it to the chosen object and then varnish. It is a pastime that can be enjoyed by both adults and children alike and some stunning effects can be produced. Tired household items such as boxes, picture frames, candlesticks, watering cans, vases and endless other objects can be easily decorated using decoupage.*

## HISTORY OF DECOUPAGE

The French verb découper means 'to cut out' and decoupage is the term now applied internationally to this craft which can be traced back to the time when paper was first introduced in the twelfth and thirteenth centuries.

Throughout this period, paper cutouts were used in Europe but the art of decoupage as we know it today, really had its origins in the late seventeenth century in Italy. It was at this time that there was a love for chinoiserie (objects or furniture decorated in the Chinese style). These were usually hand-painted and highly lacquered and there was an enormous demand, especially in Venice. In order to keep abreast with the quantities required, a new technique was introduced to imitate lacquer ware and this was decoupage. The whole process was considerably reduced in cost through copying the original piece of furniture by making it in papier mâché. This would then be covered in gesso, which in turn would have hand-tinted prints pasted to the surface which craftsmen had mass-produced from

their original designs. Finally, the furniture would have up to 30 coats of varnish applied so that the object would emulate the original lacquered furniture which came from the Orient. This art form became more popular than the very one it was trying to imitate and became known as Art Provo.

Meanwhile, in Britain, another form of decoupage was developing due to a thriving papier mâché industry and this was known as japanning. Many of the designs were similar to the original Chinese lacquer work, but the quality was thought to be superior and they were applied to papier mâché, wood, leather and tin. There was a wealth of material published during the eighteenth century using different methods such as engraving and etching, which had long been established, stone lithographs, aquatints and mezzotints, providing the decoupeur with a wide choice of subject matter.

At the beginning of the nineteenth century, purpose-made scraps first appeared which were usually black and white engravings that were often tinted. These then became more elaborate and were sometimes embossed, giving a three-dimensional

appearance to the object. The printing and embossing processes by which these were manufactured soon became automated, which meant that the volume of available scraps increased tremendously, and during the Victorian period these became an integral part of various pastimes.

Precut scraps also started to be produced so that the laborious task of cutting out every image was removed. The subject matter was usually sentimental and romantic, with angels, fans, flowers, well-dressed ladies and angelic children being the most well-liked. Military and naval themes were also very popular and scraps were used to cover entire surfaces of trunks, boxes, tins and trays.

Queen Victoria was an avid collector of scraps, as were children of the period for whom special editions of cutouts were introduced, featuring nursery rhyme characters, fairy tales, animals and alphabets. A wide range of seasonal scraps were also produced, for example celebrating Christmas, with Santa Claus being much favoured, together with angels, children and winter scenes.

Decoupage remained popular in Germany, France (where these cutouts were called 'chromos'), and America where they were known as 'swags'.

In the early twentieth century, the editor of Paris *Vogue*, Caroline Duer, was responsible for the American interest as she produced some particularly fine examples of decoupage which can still be seen today. She worked, with great panache in the mid-nineteenth-century German Biedermeier style, using gold braid, paper, flowers and embossed paper.

The huge increase in interest for decoupage during the last few years means that these scraps still sell well despite the fact that there is a vast array of materials which can be utilized to create some interesting work. Magazines, posters, packaging, postcards, used cards, wrapping paper and the use of the photocopy machine to copy, enlarge and reduce in size thousands of images means that today it is possible to create a contemporary piece of attractive decoupage very easily in the home in a weekend.

# WHAT YOU WILL NEED

You will probably find that you have a lot of the equipment for decoupage lying around your home but if not, most of those things that are necessary are inexpensive and fairly widely available.

## BRUSHES

Paintbrushes come in a variety of widths and so the area of the surface being painted will determine the size needed. It is advisable to buy the best quality you can afford as work can be ruined by stray hairs being caught in paint or varnish. These brushes are particularly suitable for oil-based paints and varnish but can obviously be used for many purposes. Artist's brushes are useful for hand-tinting prints and if acrylic paint is to be used. It is advisable to keep brushes separate once used. Use white spirit to clean your brushes unless water-based paints are being used in which case ordinary water will clean them successfully.

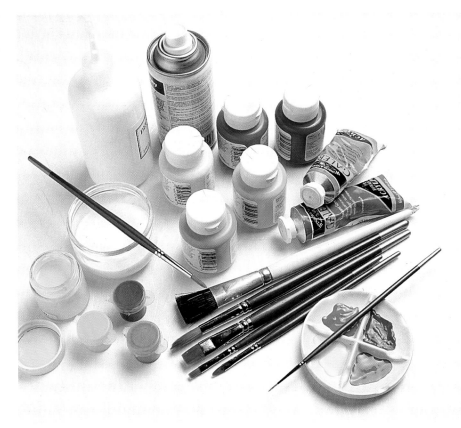

## GLUES

• **PVA GLUE** This glue is sometimes referred to as white glue and is inexpensive. It dries reasonably quickly and has a clear finish. It can be watered down and also used as a varnish.

• **SPRAY ADHESIVES** These are very clean, fast to use and do allow some movement when first applied to the object. They must be used in a well-ventilated room and directed carefully over a piece of scrap paper ①.

• **WALLPAPER PASTE** This is a slower drying glue than PVA and so has the advantage of allowing you to alter the position of the image if necessary. It also allows more time for smoothing out any wrinkles that may occur and is very cheap.

• **WOOD GLUE** Use when applying motifs to wooden surfaces.

## METHYLATED SPIRITS

This can be used with wire wool (see overleaf) when preparing the surface of an object and it is also useful for removing any excess polish. Methylated spirits can be added to shellac to dilute it and it is useful for cleaning brushes.

## OBJECTS SUITABLE FOR DECOUPAGE

The starting point for decoupage is the choice of object you wish to decorate and this can be of any age and be made from a variety of materials, as long as the surface is hard. Decoupage can give a new lease of life to many old, shabby-looking items such as tea caddies, biscuit tins, trays, vases, bowls, boxes, etc. Likewise, a paper surface such as a shoe or chocolate box presents no problems, and metal surfaces are very

successful too — jugs, plates, buckets and empty tins. Furniture, floors, walls and doors are a challenge as the area to cover is obviously larger, but the end result is very effective. It is also fun to go into junk shops to find objects to decoupage, or you can buy new containers such as boxes, tins, picture frames ② and small chests. Occasionally there are advertisements in women's magazines for hat boxes, and your local hardware store is likely to have quite a supply of galvanized metal containers such as watering cans, buckets, coal scuttles and enamelled, wooden or terracotta objects.

## PAPER SEALERS

The quality of the paper that you may use to decoupage with will vary enormously, and some papers may bleed or discolour before being applied to the surface of an object if it is not sealed first. The use of a sealant, then, will prevent discolouration and make the image very much easier to handle. Wait for the sealant to dry before cutting out the images.

• **SHELLAC OR A WHITE FRENCH POLISH** Use these products to cover an image before it is cut out. Shellac will make the paper transparent when first applied but will dry to a clear finish. French polish is also sometimes sold as button polish.

• **PRINT FIXATIVE SPRAY** This may be used as a sealant, resulting in a rubber-based coating.

## PAINTS

To a certain extent, the object selected for decoupage will dictate which paint to use, but it is worth noting that water-based paints are easier to use. Oil-based paints usually produce a more brilliant colour and can be thinned with the use of white spirit to make them easier to use, but they are also more expensive to buy.

• **ACRYLIC PAINTS** These are quick drying, water-based and can be applied over emulsion or oil-based paints. They produce very strong colours and are available in little tins or tubes from craft shops. Once the decoupage has been applied, acrylic paint is useful to add extra decoration.

• **ARTIST'S OIL PAINTS** These are expensive and should be used sparingly just to add tints with crackle glaze.

• **EMULSION PAINTS** These water-based paints can be thinned by adding water and are relatively quick drying. Several coats will need to be applied and they make a good base for decoupage.

• **GLOSS PAINTS** These are oil-based and come in a matt, eggshell or gloss finish. They can be thinned with white spirit and give a tougher finish. Twenty-four hours should be left between coats.

• **METAL PAINTS** These come in a wide range of colours and are best used on metal surfaces.

• **PRIMER** New and stripped wooden surfaces will need a coat of primer to prevent the paint from being absorbed into the grain. New metal objects will also need priming either with a red oxide or special metal primer which can easily be purchased from a decorator's shop ③.

• **UNDERCOAT** Undercoat should be used on primed, unvarnished wood.

## RESOURCES FOR SCRAPS AND CUTOUTS

There is a vast array of printed material available to the decouper today but it will take a little time to build up a supply. It is advisable to save anything you come across which you find attractive so that when the right object comes along you have your own resources to draw upon. It is a good idea to have several different folders or boxes so that when you decide to keep a scrap it can be filed under, say, flowers, cherubs, sea/shells, or any other area of your choice.

It is useful to keep postcards, Christmas and birthday cards, gift wrapping, magazines, catalogues and manuals. A good supply can be found in museums and galleries where you may also come across old charts, drawings, sketches and even old books. Books are a wonderful resource and images can be photocopied in black and white as well as colour and can be enlarged or reduced in size.

The original Victorian scraps are regularly reproduced and these can be obtained by mail order, although many can also be found in museum and craft shops. Traditionally, black and white images were used for decoupage and these were sometimes hand-tinted; take

colour photocopies if this is your only supply. It is worth remembering that there can be a greyness if using a photocopy, so be careful to select the correct paint.

## ROLLERS

These are useful for rolling over the glued paper once it is in position on the surface. It ensures there is no trapped air, removes any excess glue and irons out any wrinkles. Alternatively, use your fingers for smaller areas, or a clean, soft cloth.

## SANDPAPER AND WIRE WOOL

These are needed when preparing a surface before gluing begins and for sanding down paint and varnish between coats. Both abrasives are available in several grades ranging from fine to coarse.

## SCALPEL OR CRAFT KNIFE

These are necessary for cutting a straight line, border or any intricate detail. It is important that the blade is sharp and is replaced if there is a nick or it is blunt, or the edge of the image that is being cut will be rough. It is useful to have a special cutting mat ④ when using a scalpel, but a thick piece of card will protect a surface if this is not possible.

## SCISSORS

You will need the sharpest pair of manicure scissors you can find and the better the quality the easier the cutting will be. It does not matter if the scissors have a straight or curved blade ④.

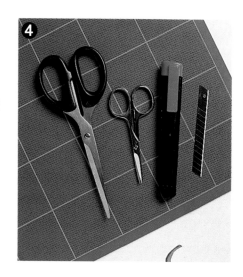

## WATERCOLOURS AND COLOURED PENCILS

The easiest way to colour a print which has been reproduced in black and white is to use watercolours or coloured pencils. Watercolours can be bought very cheaply and layers of colour can be built up making sure each layer is thoroughly dry before the next is applied. To paint with a single colour, use different depths of the same colour, starting with a thin wash over the complete image. More colour can then be added and the lighter areas painted, and so on until the darkest areas of the image are painted with the colour plus a little added black.

Likewise, when using coloured pencils, gradually build up the image, lightly shading to begin with and then creating more of a density as you proceed. Once you have finished, cover all the pencil work with a beige coloured pencil to blend the whole surface together.

## VARNISHES

• **ACRYLIC VARNISH** This is more expensive than ordinary varnish but will not yellow with age and is available with a matt or gloss finish.

• **COLOURED VARNISH** An aged look can be created using oak or antique pine varnishes. The varnish needs to be applied and then rubbed off, leaving a residue behind.

• **CRACKLE VARNISH** This gives the work an ancient, cracked look. Use two varnishes which work against each other so that one dries slowly and the other rapidly.

**⑤**

• **POLYURETHANE CLEAR WOOD VARNISH** This can be bought from decorator's suppliers and comes in clear, yellow and tinted shades. It has different finishes so that it can give a high gloss, satin or matt effect ⑤, depending on which you favour, and if painted over all of the object it will give a lasting finish to your decoupage.

## WAX

Waxing is the final coat given to the decoupaged surface and is available as beeswax as well as a number of other finishes. It should only be applied when the surface is completely dry. The first coat should be thick and left for a couple of hours before being polished followed by one or two thinner coats.

## WOOD FILLERS

It is good to have a quick drying wood filler to hand. It fills cracks, rough surfaces and small holes.

# PREPARATION OF SURFACES

The first stage with decoupage is the preparation of the surface and although this may be tedious it is worth doing well as it can affect the quality of the finished item tremendously.

## CERAMIC

Ceramic surfaces are ideal for working on but you must ensure that they are dust free. New terracotta pots or plaques can be lightly sanded and sealed with a water-based varnish which will provide the key for adhesive.

## METAL

Old metal that has rust on must be treated otherwise the rust will eventually reappear and spoil the finished decoupage. Rub down flaking and loose metal and then remove it with a wire brush, heavy duty steel wool or coarse sandpaper ①. The object should then be washed with a solution of half vinegar and half water and thoroughly dried. To ensure the piece remains rust-free, prime the surface with two coats of rust-resistant

**①**

paint or a red oxide. You can buy an all-in-one rust-proofer and primer and in this case follow the manufacturer's instructions.

New metal should always be washed either with water and detergent or with the vinegar and water solution mentioned above. The metal surface must then be thoroughly dry before applying the two coats of red oxide or an oil-based primer. This procedure must be followed for enamel, tin or any galvanized metal objects being prepared for decoupage.

## WOOD

Old wood must be sanded and cleaned thoroughly whether it has been painted, varnished or waxed. Clean the surface with detergent and water and fill any holes with a wood filler. When dry, sand the object with a medium grade sandpaper so that the surface is completely smooth.

When stripping a piece of furniture or object completely, you can always go to a commercial wood stripper but if you prefer to do the stripping yourself, buy a bottle of paint stripper or try wire wool soaked in methylated or white spirit. Once the surface has been stripped and sanded, seal it with a coat of shellac or wood primer.

New wood can be sealed with a coat of primer or undercoat but if the grain of the wood and natural colour is important to the appearance, coat it with shellac. This must then be lightly sanded to provide a key for adhesive to stick easily.

## PAINTING THE BACKGROUND

Many objects will need a base colour on which to be glued and at least two coats will be needed. Emulsion paint is ideal for covering the object you are working on and this can be diluted with a little water before being applied to the surface with a normal household paintbrush. After each coat, allow time for it to dry properly and sand lightly before applying the second layer. Oil-based paint can be used for this stage if you prefer and it is advisable if an object will get a lot of use as it will be less likely to chip than emulsion. Again it can be diluted, but this time with turpentine or white spirit.

## CUTTING AND PREPARING THE SCRAPS

The surface of all paper used for decoupage must be sealed before cutting out as this will prevent discolouration and also make it much easier to cut delicate pieces (see paper sealers on page 80).

Cut out the scraps as accurately as possible with small sharp scissors ① and/or a scalpel or craft knife. Embroidery scissors are very good for particularly fiddly pieces. When using the scalpel or craft knife, place the image on a cutting mat so as not to damage the surface beneath ②. You will also need a larger pair of scissors to cut the paper into manageable sizes before cutting the more intricate parts of the image. Inevitably, all pictures

used will be printed on different weights of paper, but as a rule remember that the best results are achieved using paper that is as light as possible.

## DESIGNING

When working on a flat object it is easy to place the cutout scraps on the surface and rearrange them until the whole composition is satisfactory. However, this is not always possible — especially when the surface is fixed and vertical or curved. When confronted with this situation, use reusable adhesive ③ or non-contact repositioning glue which will allow you to remove any images and alter their position. When you are satisfied with the composition, each image can be lifted and glued into place.

If you want to entirely cover a surface with motifs that overlap each other you will need to work out your design in a slightly different way. Start at the top and gradually work downwards. When the design feels right, make a note of the position of each scrap by taking a photograph or making a sketch. You can then remove the images, starting at the bottom and moving upwards so that the top pieces can be stuck into place first.

## GLUING

The scraps can be stuck down permanently with either PVA or wallpaper paste. A paste allows more time for you to reposition an image if necessary as it is slower drying. The glue should always be applied to the surface of the object rather than the scrap as this is less messy and if the paper is a little fragile then less handling is involved. Press down the image firmly working outwards from the centre to remove any air bubbles ④. A roller may be a useful tool at this stage for eliminating air bubbles and it can help with any creasing that may have occurred.

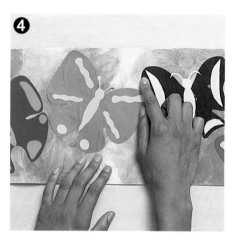

When the gluing has been completed, leave it to dry for half an hour before wiping any excess glue off the surface with a warm, wet cloth. However, if you are using PVA, wipe over the surface immediately as this adhesive dries hard. Occasionally wrinkles occur, particularly when the paper is extremely thin but these will disappear when everything is dry. Check that the edges do not begin to curl up while drying is taking place and if they do, apply a tiny amount of glue with a cocktail stick. When an air bubble does occur, pierce the bubble with a very sharp blade to allow the air to escape and then fill the incision with a small amount of glue. Leave the object to dry for a further two hours.

If you want to build up layers of decoupage to give a three-dimensional effect, paint on one layer of PVA adhesive to protect the work to date.

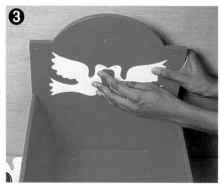

Leave to dry and then lightly sand over the surface ⑤. This may result in a white sheen but don't worry about it as subsequent layers of decoupage and PVA glue or varnish will cover it up. To finish the piece, tick on the next layer of decoupage, as before ⑥.

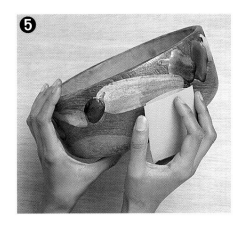

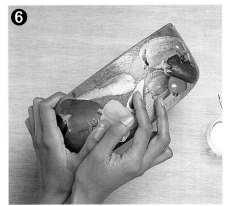

## VARNISHING

When varnishing, you must always work in a dust-free, well-ventilated space. The brush used to apply the varnish should be of good quality so that hairs will not shed, spoiling the surface of the work.

Apply as many coats of varnish as you like from three up to twenty,

depending on the quality of finish that is desired. The first layer of varnish should be thin and applied evenly with a smooth finish ⑦. It should then be left for approximately two hours before brushing on the next layer. Varnishes dry quite rapidly these days so it is possible to put on four or five layers during the course of a day.

Lightly sand the penultimate coat although it is advisable not to do this unless at least six coats have been applied. The top layer can be shiny or matt depending on the finish desired. However, it is worth remembering that a matt varnish will give a cloudy appearance after two or three coats because of the matting agent.

## FINISHING

Once the last coat of varnish has been applied the work is complete but if you want to achieve different finishes here are some further ideas with which to experiment.

### ANTIQUING
An antique or brown staining wax can be applied with a soft cloth once varnishing has been completed and this will give a mellow look once the wax

has dried and been buffed with a clean cloth. An alternative method would be to make a solution with 1 part white emulsion, 3 parts raw umber pigment and 8 parts water which is brushed on after the second coat of varnish. Wait for a minute and then rub off with a paper towel or clean cloth. Once the surface is dry continue with the next layer of varnish.

### CRACKLE VARNISH
Apply this to the top coat of varnish ⑧. The oil-based varnish is painted on first and allowed to dry before the water-based varnish is painted on top. When this is dry, the surface should look crazed but it may need a little help, in which case place the object near a lamp or radiator and this will encourage the cracking. Artist's oils, such as sienna or burnt umber, can be used to fill the cracks and are particularly effective.

### WAXING
The application of several layers of wax will give a mellow and professional look to the decoupage. It works best on top of a matt varnish which should be rubbed down with a fine wire wool before applying the wax, as directed by the manufacturer's instructions.

# ANGELS GLASS TRINKET BOX

*This pretty little box is an ideal gift to hold small pieces of jewellery. The technique used here is to stick the pictures inside the box, face down on the glass and then paint behind the images inside the box so that the box has a lustre.*

**1** Select the angels from a decoupage set, making sure that they are small enough to fit onto the sides of the box. Cut them out carefully, and trim off any excess background.

## — VARIATIONS —

Instead of these little angels, look for small pictures of shells, say, or flowers. If you are making this box as a gift for a friend, use images that you know are a particular favourite.

**2** Arrange the angels face down on the insides of the box, so that they can be seen when you look at the outside of the box. Use re-usable adhesive at first, so that you can adjust them to your liking.

**3** Stick the angels into the positions you have chosen, using the PVA adhesive and pressing them down firmly. Push out the excess glue and air bubbles by wiping over them with the soft cloth from the centre of the image outwards.

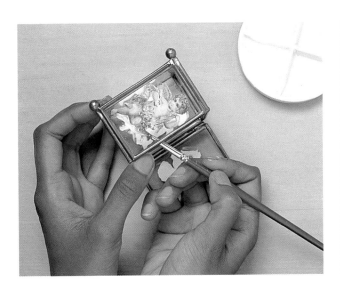

**4** Paint the insides of the trinket box and over the angels with a thin coat of PVA adhesive to seal the pictures. Allow the PVA to dry until it is only very slightly tacky.

**5** Now, paint the insides of the box with the emulsion paint. Because both the PVA and the emulsion are water-based, the tacky PVA will mix with the emulsion paint and give the sides of the box a cloudy look. Allow this to dry and then seal with another coat of PVA.

# CONTAINERS GALLERY

### Sheep box

Black line drawings of sheep have been enlarged on a photocopier and pasted onto a wooden salt box which has been painted with a dark green emulsion. Little tufts of grass were added in spring green and then the whole box was given four coats of acrylic varnish.

### Heart-shaped box

A heart-shaped plywood box has been painted black and then decorated with golden suns and moons.

### Wooden box (below)

This one is colourwashed in blue, and covered with images of the sea. It has been further decorated with embossed metal shapes made by drawing on the back of tomato purée tubes, and then cutting out using scissors.

### Fishing box (right)

A plain plywood box has been decorated with fish for a keen fisherman friend. The fish have been cut out and then painted aquamarine and blue, and the box has been washed in blue. Two fish are painted red to add some contrast to the design.

### Gift box

A box which originally contained a cake has been turned into a gift box by first painting it deep red. Images from a poster were photocopied and then the angels were cut out and touched on their rounded parts with a pink wash. The box was finally varnished with crackle varnish.

### Corrugated box

Corrugated card has become rather fashionable, but it can be a little dull. The hexagonal box used here has been embellished using corrugated card hearts some of which have been sprayed gold.

### Jewellery casket

This traditional jewellery casket was painted with coral coloured acrylic paint and then decorated with cutouts from a jeweller's catalogue. It was then painted with crackle varnish and burnt umber was rubbed into the cracks to make them show up.

# TRELLIS CANDLESTICKS

*Very delicate decoupage images can look stunning. The original concept of decoupage was to glue a cutout image onto a surface and then lacquer it until the image looked as if it was ingrained on the surface. So the more delicate or intricate the paper cutout, the more convincing the final article.*

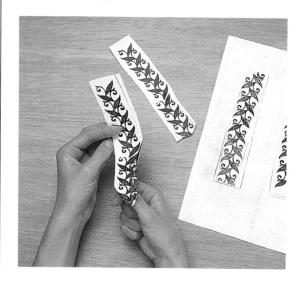

**1** Photocopy your trellis design as many times as necessary. Then with the craft knife or manicure scissors (whichever you find most comfortable to use), carefully cut out the designs. Make sure the blade is sharp, otherwise it will be difficult to cut out the intricate swirls clearly and accurately. Also cut out a number of individual leaves.

## YOU WILL NEED

| Trellis design |
| Craft knife/manicure scissors |
| Acrylic paint (black) |
| Paintbrush (fine) |
| Re-usable adhesive |
| 2 white ceramic candlesticks |
| PVA glue |
| Gloss varnish |

## VARIATIONS

Instead of positioning each piece of trellis so that it runs vertically up the candlesticks, try wrapping the trellis around the stem, winding up from the bottom to the top. You will need more pieces of trellis to achieve this, but the end result will look just like a piece of wrought iron.

2 Lay the cutouts onto a piece of scrap paper and paint over them entirely with the black acrylic paint, using the fine paintbrush. This will make the colour denser on the design; black and white photocopies can sometimes look faded and grey. Allow the paint to dry.

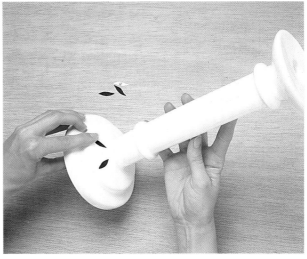

3 Using the re-usable adhesive, arrange the individual leaves around the top and bottom edges of the candlesticks. It is ideal to use a re-usable adhesive as it is easy to keep on re-arranging the leaves until you find the right composition.

4 Use re-usable adhesive in the same way for the trellis strips along the stem of each candlestick. Then stick down each piece in its chosen position using the PVA glue.

5 Varnish the candlesticks with one or two coats of the gloss varnish to finish them off. You can use the PVA glue if you prefer. It will look opaque white when you first brush it on, but it will dry to a transparent finish.

# GALVANIZED TIN WATERING CAN

*Covering tin ware with decoupage is a traditional form of this craft, and by making the images floral ones you will tie in the watering can very naturally with its surroundings in the garden. There are a great many floral gift wraps available from which you can cut your images.*

**1** If you need to, first use the wire wool to remove any rusty lumps that are on the outside of the watering can. Then wash the watering can thoroughly with warm water and detergent.

## YOU WILL NEED

| |
|---|
| Galvanized watering can |
| Wire wool |
| Detergent |
| Metal primer |
| Paintbrushes |
| Turpentine |
| Gloss paint (dark green) |
| Floral images |
| Scissors |
| Re-usable adhesive |
| PVA glue |
| Clear varnish |

### — VARIATIONS —

Vegetables or gardening implements would be equally effective and suitable on a watering can such as this. Also, don't limit yourself to the watering can, how about applying decoupage to galvanized buckets or even an old tin bath if you can find one? The decorating principal is just the same.

90

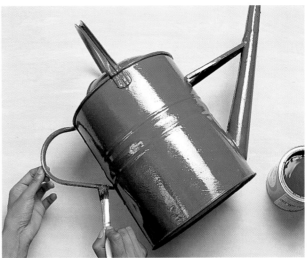

2 Once it is dry, paint the watering can with the metal primer. Be sure not to apply too thick a coat otherwise the surface on which you will decoupage may become uneven. Wash out the paintbrush thoroughly with the turpentine.

3 Once the primer is dry, paint the can all over with two coats of the dark green gloss paint, allowing the first coat to dry before you begin the next one.

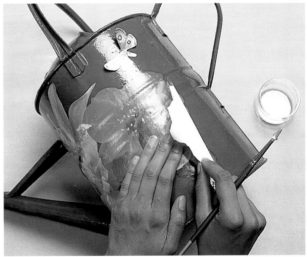

4 Cut out your chosen floral images using the scissors. The images should be quite large as smaller ones will not look as strong and clear. Arrange them on the dry watering can with the re-usable adhesive until you find a good composition.

5 Stick down the flowers with the PVA glue, pressing out the air bubbles as you go along. Stick down several layers to achieve a deeper look. Finally, apply between 10 and 12 coats of clear varnish to finish off.

# BLACK CAT
# LAMP AND SHADE

*Black cats silhouetted against a cream shade make a wonderful catty gift. Tall, stately Egyption cats, prowling fierce cats, and cosy, snuggling cats will all sit very happily side by side, united in their blackness.*

**1** Either photocopy or trace the cat silhouettes given on page 182, transfer the images onto the black sugar paper and then cut out as many of each shape of cat as you need, using either the scissors or craft knife.

## YOU WILL NEED

| Cat silhouettes (page 182) |
| Pencil |
| Black sugar paper |
| Scissors/craft knife |
| Plain lampshade and base |
| Re-usable adhesive |
| PVA glue |
| Chinagraph pencil |
| Paintbrush (fine) |
| Acrylic paint (black) |
| Gloss varnish |

### VARIATIONS

The cats needn't just be black. Perhaps you would like to recreate your own cat, if you have one, or a series of differently coloured felines. All you need to do is cut out the cat in the correctly coloured sugar paper, or paint its markings over the top of the black paper.

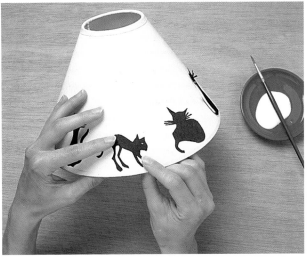

2 Using the re-usable adhesive, arrange the silhouettes around the bottom edge of the lampshade grouping them in whichever way you prefer. When you are happy with your design it is time to move onto step 3.

3 One by one, stick the cats in place using the PVA glue. To make sure they are stuck firmly, rub your fingers lightly over the top of each one to remove any air bubbles.

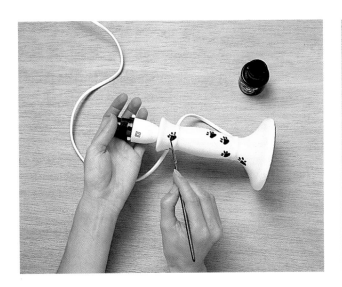

4 Using the chinagraph pencil, copy the paw prints that appear above onto the lamp base. With a chinagraph you can easily remove any mistakes you might make by simply rubbing off the marks. When the prints look right, fill in the design using the fine paintbrush and black acrylic paint.

5 To finish off the lamp base, wait until the acrylic paint has dried and then apply one or two coats of varnish to prevent the acrylic from chipping. Wait for the first coat of varnish to dry before applying the next.

# GIFTS FOR THE HOME GALLERY

### Lampshades
Globe artichokes and red tomatoes have been simply cut out and evenly arranged around a lampshade with green edging to make a very stylish accessory.

### Floral tray (right)
The tray has been sanded down and sprayed gold. The cream, white and yellow flower scraps were then chosen to complement both the gold and green of the background.

### Kitchen scales
These old-fashioned kitchen scales were rubbed down with wet and dry paper prior to painting and covering with decoupage.

### Glass biscuit barrel
The scraps of fruit stuck onto the inside of this barrel were sealed with a coat of PVA glue and then coated with two coats of pale green emulsion paint and finally a coat of dark green emulsion.

### Storage jars
Even storage jars can be made to look more interesting by covering them with decoupage. The chillies on this jar were colour photocopied and reduced to fit. Because you can see through the glass, the back of each motif is decorated to look the same as the front.

## Napkin rings

For a fruit and flower theme, I cut out pictures of berries and leaves and used these to decoupage some napkin rings which were then given several coats of polyurethane varnish.

## Salad bowl

An old salad bowl has been rejuvenated with coats of varnish and vegetables have been added in layers to give depth to the composition.

# TOY BOX

*Kids will love this brightly coloured toy box, decoupaged with toys cut out from various catalogues. The pictures make the box a label in itself: you don't have to open it up to see what is inside. For a more personalized toy box, cut out the child's name from brightly coloured gummed squares or patterned gift wrap. Draw the letter outlines first so that you know they are all the same size.*

**1** Paint the box sides alternately yellow and orange, and do the same with the box lid. Paint two to three coats leaving each coat to dry before applying the next to make the finish nicely smooth.

96

## YOU WILL NEED

Square wooden box with lid

Emulsion paints (orange, yellow)

Paintbrush

Pictures of toys

Scissors

Re-usable adhesive

PVA glue

Polyurethane wood varnish

## VARIATIONS

Instead of scattering the motifs all over the sides, why not build them up from the bottom edges so that it looks as though the toys are piled up high inside.

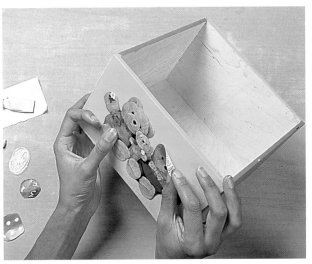

2 Cut out some pictures of brightly coloured toys from magazines or catalogues. Make sure that you have a mixture of sizes — the border of the lid, for example, will need smaller pictures, while the sides can take larger toys.

3 Arrange the pictures around the box and its lid, using the re-usable adhesive. In this way, you can re-adjust the pictures until you have designed a composition that you are happy with.

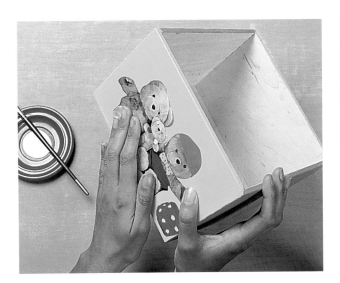

4 Stick the pictures in position using the PVA glue and smooth out any air bubbles with your fingers so that the images are well attached.

5 Varnish the entire box and lid with the polyurethane varnish. Give it three to four coats allowing each one to dry before applying the next so that the end result is tough and durable.

# BUTTERFLY FRIEZE

*This charming frieze is made very simply using brightly coloured sticky paper squares. The shapes are cut out using outlines given at the back of this book and then they can, of course, be stuck in place very easily. Mix together all the brightest colours to make a most exotic species of butterfly. Vary the sizes of the butterflies, too, so that you have some large ones and some small ones.*

**1** Water down the blue paint and wash the border using a fat paintbrush in a circular motion to create the cloudy effect shown in the photograph above.

## YOU WILL NEED

Watercolour paint (blue)

Paintbrush

20 cm (8 in)-wide border paper

Butterfly templates (page 181)

Tracing paper

Pencil

Brightly coloured gummed paper

Scissors

Re-usable adhesive

Varnish

## VARIATIONS

These gummed paper squares come in so many bright colours that you can create any picture you want in this way. Piles of different kinds of fruit, the sky at night, teddy bears in all manner of poses — let your imagination run riot and you will soon be filling friezes with an endless variety of designs.

2 Trace the templates on page 181. Then fold your gummed paper in half, transfer the template outlines onto the back of the paper and cut out to give two wings of exactly the same size. To transfer the outline, draw thickly over the butterfly outline on the back of the tracing paper, position the tracing on the folded gummed paper and then draw over the top once more.

3 In contrasting colours, make the butterfly bodies and wing patterns in exactly the same way as for the butterfly wings described in step 2.

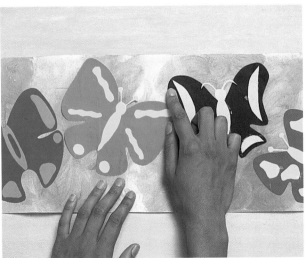

4 Dampen the bodies and wing patterns with a little water and attach onto the wings mixing the colours as much as you like to make sure you end up with beautifully ornate butterflies.

5 Now arrange the completed butterflies onto the cloudy frieze using re-usable adhesive to position them. Once they are flying around to your liking stick them down and then cover with a coat of protective varnish; either matt or glossy.

# GIFTS FOR CHILDREN GALLERY

## Shelf unit

These shelves looked a little tired so it has been repainted and decorated with a series of fifties-style images.

## Pretend play (middle)

A child's clear plastic bag and picnic set have been decorated using sticky-backed plastic cut into flower shapes.

## Storage containers

A shoe box and folder (opposite) are both given new life by painting them and then decorating them with simple geometric cut outs.

## Decorative plates

Plates such as these can be expensive, but with a touch of emulsion paint and decoupage they can quickly be decorated to fit in with the decor of a child's room.

## Wastepaper bins

Catering-size drinking chocolate drums have been converted into bins for children's rooms: one with bold brash roses and the other with nursery rhyme characters.

# MINI WINDOW BOX

*As, more often than not, window boxes are used for growing colourful flowers throughout the summer, why not make an otherwise ordinary window box into something a little more floral? With the aid of some gift wrapping paper and gold paint, the flowery panels were very neatly defined on this box.*

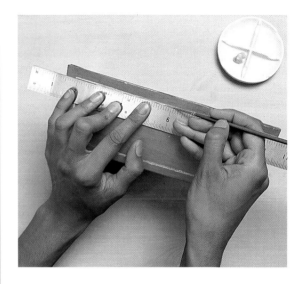

**1** Prepare the window box for decoupage by painting the outside surface with the dark red emulsion paint. Paint two or three coats for a smooth and even finish, allowing each coat of paint to dry before applying the next. Paint a narrow strip in gold paint around the edge of each side to make a panel — use the metal ruler to help regulate the lines.

## YOU WILL NEED

| |
|---|
| Small window box |
| Acrylic or emulsion paints (dark red, gold) |
| Paintbrushes (fine, medium) |
| Metal ruler |
| Scissors |
| Floral gift wrapping paper |
| PVA glue |
| Clear wood varnish |
| Sandpaper (fine) |

### TIP

Before buying the paint for decorating a window box like this, take a good look at the motifs you are going to be using and find a colour that really enhances them.

2 Carefully cut out your selected images from the floral gift wrapping paper, making sure that you cut enough to layer the images one over the other. Cut some of the flowers with straight edges so that they fit inside the gold line frame

3 Stick down the first layer with the PVA glue and then gently wipe over the top with your finger to get rid of the air bubbles. When the glue has dried, paint the flowers with clear wood varnish. Use six to seven coats, making sure that the previous coat has dried before you start on the next one.

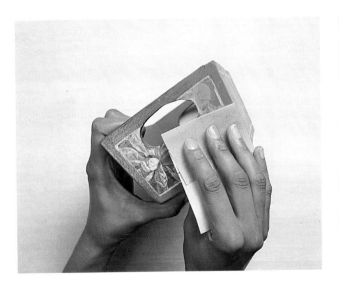

4 Using very fine grade sandpaper, sand over the varnished surface. You may find that the varnish will become opaque and white, but do not worry about this — step 5 will soon cover it up again.

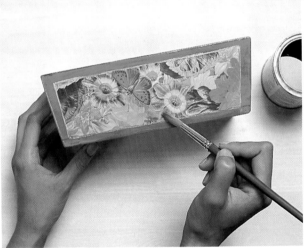

5 Glue on the second layer of flowers in the same way as step 3, and then varnish again, once more using six or seven coats of clear wood varnish. You will see that the images from beneath will become clear again. If you wish to apply more layers, repeat steps 4 and 5 until your desired effect is achieved. Brush gold paint onto the top edges of the box to give a gold stained finish.

# GIFTS FOR ADULTS GALLERY

**Wall frieze**
This frieze has been made by cutting out and sticking down squares of sticky-backed fake suede onto lining paper.

**Pencil pot**
Rather a dull pot, I painted it gold and then covered it with decoupage of gold script printed on tracing paper.

**Book cover**
This book has been treated to music stained with a tea bag.
Musical instruments have been pasted on top before varnishing.

## Wooden clock

A wooden clock kit has been decorated with overlapping gold cut outs of clocks which are printed on translucent paper.

## Mirror frame

This mock tortoiseshell mirror, a junk shop find, has been embellished by cut-outs of harps chosen because of their complementary colouring.

## Candle shades

These are easy to make and great to give away as a present. This one is decorated with decoupaged squares of sticky-backed fake suede.

## Trinket box

A small round box is a good place to keep cufflinks. This one has been painted black and the border around the lid edge has been made from scraps of paper. The crown was cut out from a magazine.

# CATS FRAME

*This frame illustrates how a picture can be built up in steps from images cut out of wrapping paper. The cat images symmetrically surround the whole of the frame, making it the purrfect frame in which to place pictures of your favourite pet.*

*This second-hand frame was quite scratched and so we first sanded it down and painted it to create a smoother surface on which to work. Always take great care to smooth down the images well as you stick them down to ensure no glue bubbles form.*

**1** Cut out lots of cats from the wrapping paper, making sure that they are small enough to fit around the frame. You may not be able to find paper exactly like this one, but there are many other commercially available gift wrapping papers with images of cats on them.

## —— VARIATIONS ——

If you are lucky enough to find a wrapping paper with cats in many different poses then you can create a more informal design on your picture frame. Scatter them around the frame always using re-usable adhesive because then you can safely keep on repositioning them until you know that you are happy with the design.

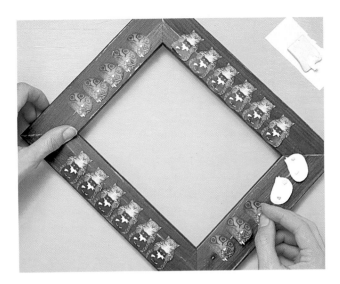

**2** Using re-usable adhesive as a temporary adhesive, arrange the cats around the frame. You can place them around randomly, but a symmetric pattern like this works very well.

**3** Also using small pieces of the re-usable adhesive, place the larger cats in each corner of the frame. Position them so that they face inwards and at an angle across the mitring.

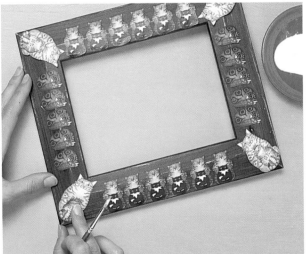

**4** Place a smaller cat on top of each larger cat, so that it looks like they are sitting in front of them. Make sure that they are both sitting on the 'ground' or the cats will look slightly strange, as though one of them were floating in the air.

**5** Stick down all the cats with PVA glue and once they are secured and the glue dried, varnish over the frame also with the PVA glue. When you first apply it, it will be white and opaque, but it will dry to a transparent finish. Two to three coats will suffice.

# TORN PAPER LEAVES FRAME

*This frame involves decorative painting as well as decoupage. Again, you don't necessarily need to use images that are available, you can just as easily create your own. Here leaves are made by tearing gummed paper into tiny leaves.*

**1** Sand the wooden picture frame all over to prepare it for painting. This will roughen the surface so that it will accept a water-based paint wash. Then mix the white paint 1:1 with water and paint on the frame. The grain of the wood will show through the white paint quite clearly.

## YOU WILL NEED

| |
| --- |
| Wooden picture frame |
| Sandpaper (fine grade) |
| Emulsion or acrylic paint (white) |
| Paintbrushes (medium, fine) |
| Gummed paper (green, two shades) |
| Acrylic paint (dark green) |
| Polyurethane satin varnish |

## VARIATIONS

In place of the leaves, perhaps you would like to make tiny bunches of grapes, say, or just hang pairs of cherries all the way around its edge. Using the same principal, tear tiny circles of paper in the appropriate colour and stick them in place grouping them closely for the grapes, or suspending the cherries from previously hand-painted stalks.

2 Rip plenty of tiny leaf-like shapes from the green gummed paper. As the paper is white on one side, when the leaves are torn, a white edge is created, giving the leaves some depth.

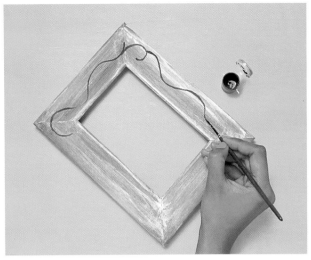

3 Using the fine paintbrush, paint a green curvy line around two sides of the frame — the top or bottom and one of the edges — with little branches coming off the main line.

4 Dampen the back of the paper leaves and secure them to the ends of the branches. Group them together in clusters, as on a tree, varying the numbers of leaves in each one to keep the design looking fluid.

5 Varnish all over the picture frame with several coats of the polyurethane satin varnish to give a shiny finish. Allow each coat to dry thoroughly before applying the next layer.

# FRAMES GALLERY

## Victorian frame

To make a Victorian style frame, a square wooden frame has been painted with blue emulsion and scraps have been stuck onto the top as a collage.

## Calligraphic frame

A plain frame has been decoupaged using torn paper with golden calligraphy and star sequins. It was then varnished with three coats of polyurethane varnish.

## Vintage car frame

For the lover of old cars, a frame decorated with vintage cars is appropriate. These images have been copied on a photocopier and then hand tinted before being stuck onto the frame and varnished.

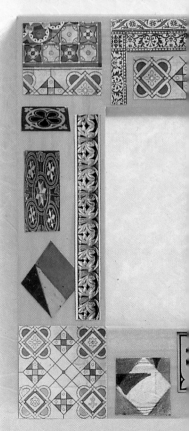

## Strawberry frame

This black frame was rubbed with gold wax and then decorated with strawberries cut out of magazines. The red and green of the strawberries contrast well with the black and gold.

## Tartan frame

This dramatic, tartan-covered frame has been dressed up still further with three silver fish and some hand-coloured Victorian engravings.

## Mosaic frame

The best decoupaged frames are those which are quite wide and allow enough room to make a bold statement. A yellow frame has been decorated in a mosaic style by cutting out shapes in complementary colours and sticking them over the frame.

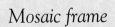

# FLOWER CRAFTS

Flowers are probably one of the most frequently given gifts, whether to celebrate, commiserate, congratulate or simply say 'thank you'. It is something of a relief that flowers always come up trumps when you're stuck for a present: they are certain to be appreciated as they always brighten up the home, whatever the season, whatever the reason. But however much a bunch of flowers is well-regarded, it can also be a little uninspired, and in *Flower Crafts*, I have endeavoured to go beyond the standard tenets of flower arranging to show just how imaginative you can be with all things floral. So although you will find some pretty posies and baskets in this book, there is also a host of really exciting and novel ways to present flowers as a gift. I have also tried to include as many different types of flowery things as possible — fresh flowers, yes, but also dried, pressed, silk, plastic and, possibly my favourites, parchment.

It has been the relatively recent development and improvement of artificial flowers and foliage which has been such an inspiration to me. Fake no longer means cheap and nasty. Instead, manufacturers are producing blooms and leaves of startling beauty. Some are very realistic, others are stylized, and they have expanded the floral designer's repertoire considerably.

Floral design is hugely enjoyable, very creative and immensely satisfying. You need only a minimum of skill (the flowers themselves really do the work), experience and equipment. The main criterion is an appreciation of flowers. If you are not able to grow your own, I have included tips on getting the best from fresh flowers, how to help them last as long as possible and how to dry, press or preserve those for other displays.

The projects cover a wealth of ideas from traditional bouquets and baskets to wreaths and wedding pendants. Some gallery items combine other craft techniques such as papier mâché, stencilling or decoupage, all of which are explained and illustrated in the "getting started" section. There are also projects and a gallery dedicated to weddings, and I hope you will feel confident enough to make some of these as your own bridal gift.

The projects are all clearly illustrated and easy to follow, but I hope you will be inspired to adapt and develop them as you want, to stamp them with your own style which is the hallmark of a gift that really is that little bit special.

# GETTING STARTED

*There are very few hard and fast rules about flower arranging, and if you're looking to create gifts which make use of silk or parchment flowers, you will not have to worry much at all. In this chapter, we look at the principal elements of floral design: fresh flowers and traditional flower arranging techniques, as well as drying, pressing, wiring and other useful floristry tips. Whatever preconceptions you might have, you do not need to spend a lot of money on elaborate equipment, and many of those that are discussed here can be found in any average home.*

## MATERIALS AND EQUIPMENT

### CHICKEN WIRE OR WIRE MESH

This can be bought from any hardware or DIY store in various gauges. Alternatively, you can buy floral wire mesh which is plastic coated and kinder to your hands. The former is cheaper, but you will need to wear gloves to handle it. It can be cut with wirecutters, secateurs or pliers. Use it for making wreath bases, topiary shapes or pendants.

### FLORIST'S FOAM

This the mainstay of flower arranging. It is available for fresh flowers (generally green) and for dry arrangements (grey). The foam for fresh flowers must be soaked thoroughly in water before use and sprayed regularly with fresh water to keep the flowers healthy. This type of foam holds a lot of water, so don't just run it under the tap; although it may appear completely wet, it is unlikely to have had the chance to absorb sufficient water.

Florist's foam comes in a variety of different shapes: spheres, rounds and bricks are the most popular, but you can also buy garlands, posy holders and other shapes used by professional florists for funerals or weddings.

Both wet and dry foam can be cut down to any size or shape with a large, dull-bladed knife. Dry foam is quite unpleasant to the touch and it is advisable to wear thin gloves if you have sensitive skin.

### FLORIST'S SOFT CLAY

This is rather like soft modelling clay, which does not harden and which can be used for fresh and dry flower arrangements. It is wedged into the base of the container and the flower stems are pushed into it to hold them in place. It is also used to stick pinholders or small prongs to the base of a container.

### GLUE GUN

This little electric, trigger-operated hobby gun is perfectly adequate for most floral projects. The glue is inserted as a solid stick into the back of the gun. The glue then melts and can be squeezed on to the item you want to stick. For anyone unfamiliar with a glue gun it is a tremendous asset, as you will no longer need to hold on to two sticky items while waiting for them to adhere. However, the glue is very hot and can burn. The glue also dries very rapidly, so be sure of where you want to place your item first.

### PINHOLDERS

These sit at the base of a container and vary from plastic prongs on which florist's foam is impaled, to the spiky metal versions that are used to hold flower stems in place.

### SECATEURS AND SCISSORS

Secateurs are really useful for cutting wire as well as pruning the roses: which means that they are very handy if you are planning on using parchment flowers which come on stiff wires. Strong, sharp kitchen scissors are good for just about everything else, although if you want to tackle decoupage (see page 123) you will need a smaller pair.

### TAPES

The most common floral tape is gutta percha — a green, white or brown, stretchy tape which is used to bind flower stems together. It is immensely useful and can be called into service whenever any types of flowers need to be bound together. Other floral tapes include an adhesive version for sticking florist's foam to a container and the papery green tape that is used for binding a buttonhole or creating an artificial stem.

### WIRE

Florist's wire is sold as stub wire (in various thicknesses or gauges — medium gauge is suitable for most things) and reel wire. The former comes in bunches of cut lengths of wire that are between about 15 and 25 cm (6 and 10 in) long. It is used for numerous floral tasks. An investment in one bunch of medium gauge wires will probably be all you need. Reel wire is thinner and, as you would presume from its name, comes on a reel. It is used really in place of twine or string, or where a fine finish is required (a buttonhole, for example).

German pins are U-shaped pieces of thick wire (rather like old-fashioned hair pins) which are used to secure moss or other items to florist's foam.

# FRESH FLOWERS

Always choose the very best flowers, whether you grow your own or buy from a florist. Look for fresh, new blooms with crisp foliage. Avoid flowers or buds which have browning petals or where foliage is drooping or discolouring. Sometimes, although not always, it is worth paying a little extra for the benefits of a good florist shop where the flowers are well cared for and sold in peak condition, rather than the cheaper market stall. Having said that, I have been pleasantly surprised by market flowers, and even those bought by the roadside, and very disappointed with expensive blooms. Conditioning the flowers when they arrive home is probably the best advice, wherever they come from.

### CONDITIONING

For cut flowers to last, they must be conditioned. This will enable them to absorb maximum water right up to the flowerheads. Obviously, some varieties last better than others, but all flowers will die quickly unless cared for. If you want long-lasting varieties, try chrysanthemums, carnations, lilies, gypsophila, statice, alstroemeria and golden rod. Varieties with slightly less longevity, but still guaranteed to give you several days life, include: roses

(although hothouse varieties in winter rarely open or last very long), gerberas, tulips, narcissi and delphiniums.

To condition your flowers, first strip away the foliage on the lower part of the stems ①. Any leaves below the waterline will rot, and any rotting matter will encourage bacteria which

will cause the plant to die rapidly. Then cut at least 5 cm (2 in) from the end of the stem with sharp scissors, cutting at an angle ②. With very woody stems, like roses, use a sharp knife to slice up the stem end another 5 cm (2 in). This will ensure maximum water absorption. Place the trimmed flowers into a cool place, in a deep container of water.

Some plants may require a little more assistance. Sunflowers, for example, should be totally immersed in water (lay them in a bath); while tulips and other flowers with hollow stems may develop air bubbles in the stem, causing the plant to droop alarmingly. One way to disperse this is to turn the plant upside down, fill it with water, place your thumb over the end and insert into a container of water ③. If the plant still wilts (tulips are notorious for this), prick a pin through the stem just under the flowerhead.

Once arranged, avoid placing the flowers near fruit. Experts have discovered that ripening fruit (particularly bananas) emits an ether which has a disastrous effect on cut flowers causing them to wilt.

Any flowers arranged in florist's foam will need a daily drink of fresh water, otherwise the foam will dry out and the flowers will die.

# DRYING FLOWERS

If you're in a hurry, most florists now stock a range of dried flowers to buy; although the quality will vary from place to place. Always choose freshly-dried specimens and avoid dusty, faded ones. However, with many flowers it is simplicity itself to dry your own. Rows of hanging, drying flowers can also look decorative in themselves, giving an added dimension to a kitchen or utility room.

There are basically three ways to preserve flowers:

### AIR DRYING

This is the simplest and works for quite a lot of flowers. Use this method for roses, peonies, hydrangeas, statice, sunflowers, seedheads, helichrysum and

helebores and geraniums can all be dried in this way. You will need to buy silica gel (which is actually crystals), borax or silver sand from a hardware store or chemist. Place the crystals or powder in an airtight container. Lay the flowers on top and gently cover with more crystals/powder ③. Make sure the plants are completely covered. Now cover with a tight-fitting lid and leave. If you are using silica gel, check after two or three days. To test, gently shake back the crystals and touch the petals, they should feel slightly tissuey and leathery. (Some crystals change colour as they absorb moisture, and this will also be an indicator as to when the

sunray (helipterum). Simply bunch a few stems together (not too many, as air should be allowed to circulate between the flowerheads. If the flowerheads are too clustered, they may go mouldy and brown). Wind a rubber band around the end of the stems ① and hang the flowers upside down from a butcher's hook (or similar) on a clothes drying rack, bookcase or shelf in a place well out of sunlight. Avoid steamy areas, or any room which is not warm and completely dry. Sunlight will strip your flowers of all colour really quickly.

Flowers will take up to three weeks before they are dry. To test, turn the flowers back up the right way; the stem should completely support the flowerhead. If it droops even slightly, or feels soft to the touch, the plant isn't quite ready and will need longer.

Hydrangeas and delphiniums can also be dried by standing them upright in a little water. When the water has been absorbed, leave the plants standing where they are until dry.

Dried petals, especially those from roses, make lovely confetti or potpourri. To do this, lay out the petals on some newspaper or brown wrapping paper ②. Cover with another sheet of paper and weight down *gently* with two or three newspapers. After a week, they should be ready to use

## DRYING WITH DESICCANTS
Some specimens need to have the moisture drawn from them. Narcissi, camelias, carnations, fuchsias, lilies,

plants are ready). Borax and silver sand will take longer to work — around 10 days or so.

You can speed up this process by placing your container (with silica gel and without the lid) in a microwave oven. Put in a small cup of water beside your container and blast on full power for between 1 and 4 minutes. (Denser blooms will take longer than fragile, single petalled varieties.) If you want to try this method it is worth experimenting as all microwave ovens vary, and so do the plants you use. Time and practice will yield the best results.

## PRESERVING WITH GLYCERINE

This is the method used to preserve foliage. Although I haven't used any preserved leaves in this book, it is worth knowing how to do this, as the foliage will last for many, many months (even years) because the glycerine gives the leaves a supple, leathery appearance.

Use late spring or early summertime foliage, when the plant is still taking up water (in autumn, it will stop!). Mix up one part glycerine to two parts very hot water. Allow the solution to cool. Cut the stems at a sharp angle and stand in about 8 cm (3 in) of the cooled glycerine solution. As the plant begins to absorb the glycerine, the leaves will change to a dark, coppery colour. Any glycerine sweat beads which form can be wiped from the leaves. Check every week or so until the leaves have changed colour and are supple and leathery to the touch.

# PRESSING FLOWERS

Pressing flowers is a well established hobby. It is a wonderful way to capture the beauty and fragility of a plant without losing any of its colour. It is also a lovely method of preserving wild flowers, which are usually too fragile to last as cut flowers and which generally do not dry well.

Pick flowers around midday when all the dew has evaporated and the plant has taken up sufficient water. Lay gently in a basket and press as soon as possible. If you want to pick wild

flowers, it is worth putting them into a plastic bag which, if you blow up like a balloon, will keep the flowers in a satisfactory state until you return home. You do not need a flower press, although if you enjoy pressing flowers, you will no doubt want to make or buy one as generally they are more manageable and easier to use. Instead, you can use heavy books and layers of tissue paper and cardboard (although with this latter method you will need to affix 'do not touch' notes to prevent unsuspecting members of the household from disturbing the pile!).

Take a piece of tissue paper and lay the flowers or leaves on top, leaving sufficient space around each one. (Multi-petalled flowers will need breaking down into smaller parts for pressing, but single flowers can be pressed whole.) When you have filled the tissue, place another piece on top and put the whole thing in between two pieces of corrugated cardboard (for thicker specimens, it is worth adding a layer of blotting paper as well). Put the whole sandwich in between some heavy books (make sure the books are larger all around so that the flowers on the outer edges are pressed correctly). After a day or so, place another book on top of the pile. Repeat this again after another few days and again a few days later. Your flowers will take up to six weeks to dry, although some things will be usable after just two or three weeks.

# ARTIFICIAL FLOWERS

No longer the rather nasty, tatty items found in cheap cafés, most artificial flowers are fabulous imitations of their fresh counterparts. You can now choose from a huge range of fabric (called silk, although they are often not), plastic or parchment. Generally, silk flowers are cheaper than parchment, but the latter have an irresistible quality which silk are unable to match. Virtually every flower is represented artificially, which is great if you want to find daffodils in October. When mixed with fresh or dried flowers, they can be almost indistinguishable from the real thing, especially if viewed from a distance.

Artificial flowers are easy to handle, last indefinitely and because they have improved so much in recent years, are a floral designer's delight. Also available is a large range of fabric, parchment and plastic foliage, some of which is a superb copy of nature, and ideal for making garlands, headdresses and decorating gifts.

# MAKING GARLANDS

Many florists and all floral wholesalers will sell a wide range of wreaths. These vary from the rounds of dry or fresh florist's foam, through vine and twig wreaths to wire garland rings. Or make a base from twigs or chicken wire.

## CHICKEN WIRE RINGS

These are either filled with sphagnum moss (for dry arrangements) or wet foam (for fresh ones). Take a long thin rectangle of chicken wire and wrap it around a fat wad of moss or pieces of florist's foam ①. Twist the wire edges in on themselves and then mould the wire into a circle (working around your waistline is a good guide). When you have formed your circle, secure the two ends together with some stub wire ② (see picture overleaf).

## WREATH RINGS

These are sturdy wire bases which are usually covered with sphagnum moss. The moss is secured to the base by winding florist's string or twine round and round the ring to hold it in place.

**❶**

**②**

## AFFIXING FOLIAGE AND FLOWERS TO A GARLAND

What you add to a garland base is entirely up to you. Usually, a foundation of foliage is inserted first ④ and other items, such as cones, berries or flowers are added on top. If you are using a wet foam wreath, it is simple to push the stems of the plants directly into the foam. For any other type of wreath using dried or artificial plants, you can either push the wired ends of the items into the base, or stick on the pieces with a glue gun.

## FOAM RINGS

Made in different sizes, foam rings are also made from dry or wet foam.

## TWIG OR VINE WREATHS

These are very popular and look great even without anything on them. They are inexpensive to buy, but you can make your own, particularly if you are interested in basket making. Supple twigs are simply twisted around each other and secured into a ring with some heavy gauge stub wire. If you don't want a natural coloured base, you can paint it by rubbing emulsion paint on to the twigs with a cloth ③. If you buy a painted wreath, you can distress it slightly by sanding the surface with a small piece of sandpaper.

## WIRING CONES AND SEEDHEADS

Although a glue gun is immensely handy for many garland designs, occasionally it is necessary to attach a piece to a length of wire. This is especially so for fresh arrangements, where glue is inappropriate.

To wire strange shapes such as cones or seedheads, take a piece of medium gauge stub wire, bend the end into a U-shape and hook it around the base of the piece ⑤. Once the wire is hooked in place, twist the shorter end around

**③**

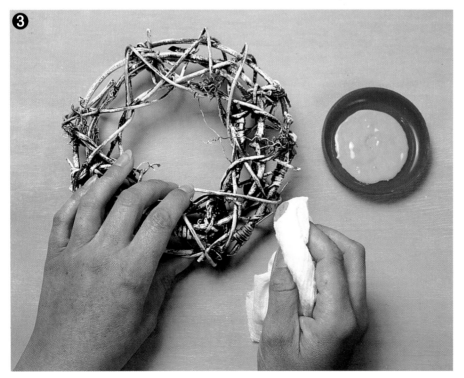

**⑤**

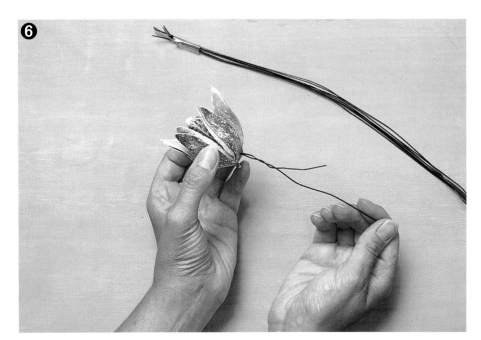

## HANGING A PENDANT OR GARLAND

Make a hanging loop with heavy gauge stub wire. Push one end of wire through the top of the garland or pendant and twist the wire back on itself to secure. Push through the other end of wire a little distance away and repeat ⑧. This secure hanging device should not show when the design is in place.

# MAKING POSIES AND BOUQUETS

A posy can be a simple gathering of garden flowers or a more formal display, swathed in tissue paper and cellophane

the longer piece to give you a tail ⑥ which you can then insert into florist's foam or a twig wreath base.

## ADDING FRUIT

The easiest way to secure fruit into an arrangement is to spear it with a wooden skewer or cocktail stick ⑦ and push this into florist's foam. If you are working on a garland, swag or pendant and glue is inappropriate, wire fruit by pushing in a piece of heavy gauge stub wire (in much the same way as you do for cones or seedheads). Twist the wire around to secure it and pull it hard so that most of the wire sinks into the flesh of the fruit and then disappears.

with a mass of shiny ribbons. Whatever type of posy or bouquet you make, here are a few simple presentation tips to help you.

## BUILDING UP A BUNCH

When you are assembling your flowers, it helps to build up a small bunch first, securing it with some floral tape ① (see picture overleaf) before adding more flowers to build up the display.

Most florists use string or floral twine, but I have always found the stretchy floral tape to be much easier to use. You only need a short length (no more than around 20 cm [8 in]) at a time. Then, to use the stretchy tape, pull it tightly and you will find the tape will cling in place neatly.

**1**

## STEM ENDS

For a natural finish, leave the stem ends of a posy showing, but make sure they are all neatly trimmed to the same length. For fresh posies or bouquets, it helps to preserve the flowers by covering the ends with a piece of cellophane or plastic wrap and then tissue paper. This prevents the ends from drying out too quickly and also provides a neat finish for any sap-oozing stems in the bouquet.

Cut a small square of cellophane or plastic wrap, fold around the end of the stems and secure with a rubber band ②. Cut a slightly larger square of white or coloured tissue paper, place the stem ends in the centre of the tissue and fasten with another rubber band which you can then cover with gift ribbon ③.

## FORMAL BOUQUETS

Don't be daunted by these more elaborate floral displays: the key is the finishing touches, like the ribbon flourish and clear floral cellophane. Buy both ribbons and cellophane from a floral supplier, although you can improvise with giftwrap ribbon from stationery stores. The flamboyant bows which usually decorate these floral masterpieces are simplicity itself, and are merely pull-up devices, needing zero skill to operate.

You can either make up your display directly on to the cellophane and then wrap it around the flowers (working either so that the cellophane is wrapped around the sides of the piece, or so that it folds over at the top of the display), or you can make up your arrangement on a worksurface and then envelop it in the cellophane.

Secure the cellophane at the base with a small piece of narrow gift ribbon. Tie this tightly and finish with a knot. This is then covered with a larger display bow and ribbon.

As a finishing touch, run a piece of matching wide ribbon up the side of the cellophane, or even along the top, and secure with staples. Add ripples of narrower ribbon over the top of the wide ribbon to cover the staples, sticking it in place with double-sided tape and curl any tail ends of ribbon with a scissor blade.

**2**

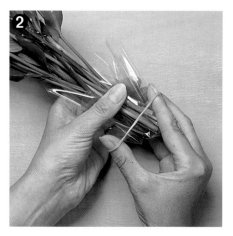

## LILIES

These fabulous florist's favourites look and smell utterly divine. However, the pollen from the exotic looking stamens is absolutely indelible and will stain furniture and clothes. It will also blemish the petals if they are brushed against. Because of this, many florists trim off the stamen ends before arranging lilies. Do this using a small pair of scissors. Hold the flower upside down so that the pollen falls off on to a scrap of paper ④.

**3**

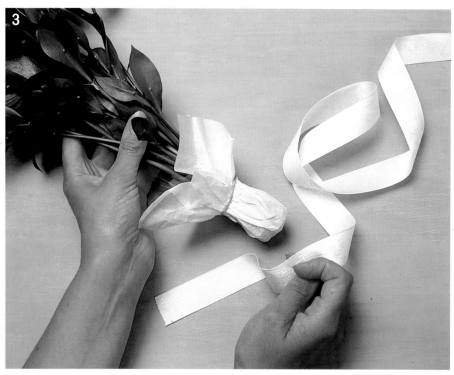

## MAKING BUTTONHOLES

To make successful buttonholes, you must invest in the green paper tape used by professional florists. This tape is slightly stretchy and will cling to itself once it has been wound round the stems of the buttonhole. It also gives a neat finish and covers any wire you might have used.

Cut one or two flowers to length (hold them against your chest to give you a more accurate idea of the length that you need). You might also, perhaps, hold a tiny piece of foliage as well ①. Secure together with a twist of reel wire, then cover the ends with the green paper tape ②. Finish with a little coordinating ribbon.

## MAKING TREES

Little mop-head or cone trees covered with moss, foliage or flowerheads are a popular gift idea and they are very easy to make. You will need a suitable pot, twigs or small branches for the trunk and a florist's foam shape (sphere or cone) for the head. Depending on the size of the tree, it can be fixed into the pot in dry florist's foam, soft clay or even set in plaster of Paris.

Hold up the pot, trunk and tree top to gauge the proportions; make sure the sizes work together and that the pot is not too big for the head or vice versa ①. Wedge florist's foam or soft florist's clay into the pot, push in the trunk (a thick and thinner piece together often look quite stylish) and squash the sphere or cone head down on top. If you are making a large tree, it is stronger if you set the trunk into plaster of Paris. You will need to fill the pot with crumpled newspaper and then a plastic bag. Pour the plaster into the plastic bag and insert the trunk. You will need to support the trunk until the plaster sets.

Decorate the tree head with flowers or leaves ② (a glue gun really comes into its own here) and pack some lichen or bun moss around the base of the trunk to cover the foam, clay or plaster.

## MAKING RIBBONS

There are so many lovely ribbons available that it is sometimes difficult to choose just one.

### PAPER RIBBON

Don't confuse this type of ribbon with the floral paper ribbons described below. It is actually much more expensive and is a relatively recent newcomer to the floral scene. It is sold in coils, often available by the metre (yard). As it is twisted round on itself, you will have to tease it open to use it. It is available in a wide choice of colours, particularly the duskier shades.

### SATIN RIBBON

Most frequently used for dress-making or other crafts, satin ribbon is widely available from department stores, fabric shops and market stalls, and makes an excellent finish for many floral designs. However, it isn't as manageable as traditional floral ribbons.

### TRADITIONAL FLORAL PAPER RIBBON

This is one of the cheapest ribbons to buy. It is available in a wide colour range, including a vast array of pastel shades. It is usually sold in 2.5 cm (1 in) widths and as the narrow 5 mm (¼ in) gift ribbon. Also available in pull-up bows, this type of ribbon can be bought from any floral supplier or well-stocked florist.

### WIRED RIBBON

Like satin ribbon, wired ribbon is also fabric ribbon which has a very fine wire stitched into both edges. This means that any bow or flourish will retain its shape. Wired ribbon often comes in lavish colours and patterns, many with a metallic tinge or glint.

### MAKING A BOW

Fold a length of ribbon into a bow shape and hold together with your fingers ①. Wind a snippet of reel wire around the centre of the bow to hold it in place ② and cover with a small piece of ribbon. Secure at the back with a piece of sticky tape.

If you want curling ribbon ends (only achievable with paper gift ribbon), so popular with giftwrapping, pull the sharp side of a scissor blade up and along the ribbon in one quick movement ③.

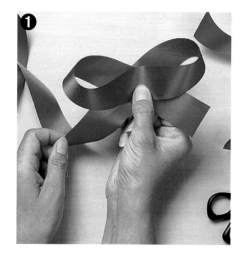

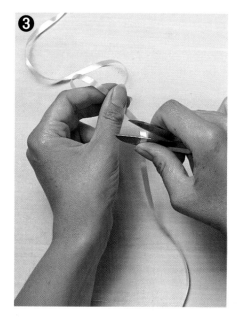

## OTHER TECHNIQUES

I have always thought of flower arranging as such a narrow term, and instead have constantly tried to push back the boundaries of how flowers and plant material of all types can be incorporated into other aspects of home style. It is great fun to experiment and combine flowers with other traditional craft techniques such as decoupage, stamping and other forms of decoration. After all, flowers and foliage have been decorative forms since decoration began, so don't feel limited to flowers in baskets, bunches or vases.

For those unfamiliar with some of these other techniques, I have given basic instructions here, although excellent books on each of these skills exist if you want to venture further.

### PAPIER MÂCHÉ

This is such a cheap and cheerful craft, and one which has grown in popularity recently. Its naive form has a particular charm, although practised artists can achieve such sophisticated effects that papier mâché can resemble pottery.

Basically, soft, gluey paper is applied to a mould and built up in layers which, when dry, is strong and durable. The papier mâché is then painted and varnished to finish off.

Use newspaper, torn into tiny strips, and dip them into a solution of flour and water paste (the consistency of

unwhipped cream). The mould to which you apply the paper strips can be cardboard (as in the case of the napkin rings on page 50 and opposite, bottom right ①), wire, clay, a bowl or a balloon. Generally, the first two types of mould stay in place when the papier mâché is complete; the latter three are removed when the papier mâché is dry, leaving you with a paper shell. Any mould which is being removed should be coated with petroleum jelly first to prevent the papier mâché from sticking.

Build up the layers (three or four is usually sufficient) and leave to dry thoroughly before giving a coat of white emulsion paint. You are then ready to decorate as you wish.

## STAMPING

This form of decoration is so simple, yet can be so effective. A stamp can be made from all manner of materials: cork, sponge, rubber, wood. The stamp is pushed onto an inked stamp pad or is painted with a layer of water-based paint before being stamped onto the item to be decorated.

Rubber stamps can be bought in hobby shops, stationers or through mail order suppliers. There are many floral motifs available. Alternatively, wooden textile printing blocks make excellent stamps and many come in floral designs, too. I used textile blocks to print the pretty potpourri bags below ②, along with a simple daisy stamp carved from a wine cork. Although you can use many

items to create stamps, floral devices are usually best bought or carved with a sharp craft knife from cork or polystyrene.

## STENCILLING

Many people are familiar with this form of embellishment, which has a big place in home decoration. Making your own stencils are easy and fun. Use clear acetate or stencil card. Trace, copy or draw your design onto some paper and transfer to the stencil material (for acetate, you can simply lay the design underneath and cut out the shape from that; card needs to be drawn on with a felt-tipped pen). The motif is cut out using a sharp craft knife. The stencil is then taped onto the item to be decorated and paint is either dabbed, crayoned, brushed or sprayed onto the stencil. When dry, the stencil is

removed and the motif will appear underneath.

Stencilling is a great way of achieving a regular repeat pattern (see the stencilled pansy pots below ③), and you can also use other household items as stencils such as lace or doilies. For example, see the Rose Frame on page 113 where doilies create a pretty edge.

Specialist stencil shops or DIY stores will sell stencil paints, crayons, pre-cut stencils, card and acetate, although the basics can also be bought from stationers.

## DECOUPAGE

This is a craft much loved by the Victorians who applied it to screens, trays and other furniture. Today, it has seen something of a revival, and once again, it is not just the traditional technique which is being employed, but other styles and variations which are broadening this craft and bringing it to a much wider audience.

Traditionally, decoupage involves cutting out pictures from books and magazines, sticking them onto any object in an attractive pattern, and sealing with several layers of glossy varnish.

To make floral gifts, you can combine pressed flowers with this traditional technique (see Decoupage Card below ④) to achieve a very unusual and delicate effect.

Use a paper glue, such as PVA and an acrylic varnish for most items.

# WINTER GARLAND

*Parchment flowers are perfect for winter garlands. They do not fade or wither, and look really elegant in almost any setting. These creamy, green peony roses are set on a white painted vine wreath against fake cotoneaster foliage and teamed with gilded paper figs and dried orange slices. It's a pleasure to have this garland hanging at any time of year, but it makes an unusual and refreshing change at Christmas.*

**1** If you can only buy a natural vine wreath, paint it white first with emulsion paint. Once dry, rub the wreath with a piece of sandpaper to distress the surface and reveal some of the natural wood that is beneath.

## YOU WILL NEED

| White painted vine wreath |
| --- |
| Sandpaper |
| Secateurs or scissors |
| Fake cotoneaster foliage |
| Reel wire |
| White parchment peony roses |
| Gold paint |
| Fake figs |
| Glue gun |
| Dried orange slices and tiny oranges |
| Heavy gauge stub wire |

## VARIATIONS

For a more traditional garland, use fake fur or pine foliage with gilded cones, clusters of artificial berries and bright red, silk poinsettias.

2 Using secateurs or scissors, cut the foliage into manageable pieces and twist them in and out of the wreath, working in one direction only, until the base is virtually covered. Make sure that you reveal some of the white wreath base though. Use lengths of the reel wire to keep the foliage in place.

3 Trim down the peony roses using secateurs or wire cutters and push the stems into the wreath. Keep the flowers at an equal distance apart, and peel open their petals once they are in position. (Parchment flowers are packaged with the petals and leaves tucked in. It's terrific fun to mould and tweak these into shape: they are much more manageable and obedient than their fresh cousins!)

4 Put a little gold paint on your finger and rub on to the fake figs to add highlights. Cut down their stems with wire cutters or secateurs and slot into the display. I have only used two bunches to add a change of texture and interest to the garland.

5 Finally, plug in the hot glue gun and once the glue has melted, stick the dried orange slices and small dried oranges in place around the wreath. Hot glue sticks rapidly, so work quickly. If you make a mistake, pull the piece off immediately, as items can be quite difficult to remove once the glue has dried. Create a hanging loop at the back of the garland with the stub wire (see page 119).

# PRESENTATION POSY

*Everyone is delighted with a posy of flowers, and this particular one will arrive in pristine condition as it is packed in a customized gift box. Hat boxes are now widely available in a range of different sizes from stores selling greetings cards and stationery. If you don't like the pattern on the box, recover it with pretty giftwrap or wallpaper to complement the flowers. Pack with shredded tissue before adding the posy.*

**1** Strip the leaves from the lower stem ends of the roses and remove any nasty thorns. Group together several stems, interspersing them with the brodiaea, and secure with florist's tape.

## YOU WILL NEED

| |
| --- |
| Pink roses |
| Blue brodiaea |
| Florist's tape |
| Scissors |
| Ruscus foliage |
| Purple net |
| Gift ribbon in lilac and deep purple |
| Purple tissue paper |

— TIP —

It is nice to cover the standard gift boxes, as you can achieve a perfect match with your flowers. PVA glue is suitable for most papers. Add a pretty bow on the box lid for a final flourish.

**2** Add in some ruscus stems, making sure that you strip off any lower leaves, so that the posy comes together tightly. Bind the posy together just beneath the flower heads with a strip of florist's tape.

**3** Continue to build up the posy, creating an even mix of roses, brodiaea and foliage. When you have added the last pieces, secure with a final piece of tape.

**4** Cut a piece of purple net into a rectangle, twice the height of the posy and long enough to wrap around it with generous folds. Wrap the net around the flowers, securing it at the stems with some of the lilac gift ribbon. Tie the ribbon in a tight knot but leave the ends trailing for the time being.

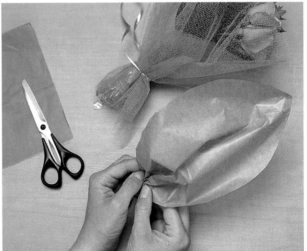

**5** Cut the tissue paper into three large leaf shapes. Take one shape at a time and pleat at the base with your fingers. Place the tissue leaves around the posy and bind with the deep purple gift ribbon. Tie the ribbon in a tight knot and leave the ends trailing. Curl the four ribbon ends using a scissor blade.

# BOUQUETS, POSIES AND GARLANDS GALLERY

## Lavender posy

For a posy which is scented as well as decorative, gather together a neat bunch of pretty little sunray (helipterum) and surround them with a well-ordered circlet of heady, fragrant lavender. Keep the flower heads level and trim the stems to the same length for a smart finish. Secure with twine or tape and cover with purple ribbon and decorative twine.

## Summertime hat

A little straw hat makes such a pleasing wall hanging. Wind narrow ribbon around the crown and leave overlong tails hanging, then trim with a circle of bright yellow strawflowers (helichrysum), sticking the flower heads in place with a glue gun.

## Gerbera bouquet

The vivid colours of gerbera always ensure a cheerful composition. Mix just four gerbera with a few daisy chrysanthemums and leather leaf fern for an informal but attractive bouquet. Finish with a frill of tissue paper and forest green satin ribbon.

## Mini cherry garland

Tiny twig wreath bases are inexpensive to buy and can be speedily transformed into a welcome present. Twist around checkered black and white ribbon, then wind a narrower red ribbon around on top. Slot in a bunch of fake cherries and leaves and add a red ribbon tied in a loose bow at the top.

## Sunflower plait

Plaited corn makes an excellent base for flower ropes and garlands. If you are unable to obtain enough stalks to plait your own, corn plaits are readily available to buy. Secure the ends at the top with heavy gauge stub wire and add a jaunty parchment sunflower, wedged into the plait.

## Delphinium wreath

Wreaths look stunning when composed of just one flower. Cut the dried delphinium flower heads into 12.5 cm (5 in) lengths. Push row upon row of them into a dried foam base, flatten each row against the base and tie them down at their tops with a piece of reel wire. Work around the wreath in one direction and finish with glossy purple ribbon in a loop at both top and bottom.

129

# CANDLE RING

*No special dinner would be complete without a spectacular centrepiece. Candles are a traditional favourite, and these tall yellow ones sit in a garland of shiny foliage, bright, crisp flower heads and mouthwatering lemons and limes. Candle rings are popular in many cultures, the circle signifying friendship. Although a fabulous piece, this candle ring should not take you more than an hour to put together.*

**1** Cut a long rectangle of chicken wire (this one was about 60 x 30 cm [24 x 12 in], although you can make this larger or smaller) and place small blocks of wet foam along its length, like a little train. Fold the wire lengthways into the centre, twisting the raw edges together to secure it. Wear the gloves when doing this as the wire is quite sharp.

## YOU WILL NEED

Chicken wire

Secateurs or wire cutters

Wet florist's foam

Gardening gloves

Few stub wires

Stems of foliage

Scissors

3–4 lemons

3–4 limes

Cocktail or orange sticks

White daisy chrysanthemums

White spider chrysanthemums

Floral candle holders

Three yellow candles

— TIP —

If you are unable to buy floral candle holders, buy plain flat ones, made either from glass or metal, and set them against the inner edges of the garland, tucking them well into the foliage so that the bases are covered.

2 Twist the wire and foam sausage into a circle, moulding it against your waist for a rounded effect. Join the two ends with some stub wires and adjust until you are happy with the circle. Begin to add short pieces of foliage, pushing the stem ends into the wet foam and working around the ring in one direction only.

3 When the wire is virtually covered both inside and out with foliage, add the fruit. These can be used whole or cut in half. Push each piece on to a cocktail or orange stick and push the stick firmly into the foam.

4 Add clusters of chrysanthemums into the arrangement, cutting their stems short and pushing them into the foam. Work around the circle in the same direction as the foliage.

5 Finally, add the candle holders. Floral candle holders have spikes so that you can push them into the foam. Set them around the ring, equidistantly and then pop the candles in place and light.

# FLOWER AND FRUIT BASKET

*A basket brimming with fresh fruit is always a well-received gift, but why not make something a little more special by bedecking the basket itself with clusters of dried flowers. Long after the fruit has been eaten, the basket can continue to be enjoyed.*

*Bear in mind that the larger the basket, the more dried flowers you will need to use. Don't skimp on the flowers though, as the effect will be spoilt. If your budget can't quite stretch to a basket of this size, make a smaller version (see Variations below).*

**1** Begin by gathering together little clusters of flowers and seedheads. Keep the clusters small, but don't cut the stems too short. Secure the clusters with a length of reel wire that is about 15 cm (6 in) long. Wind the wire around the stems two or three times and attach the cluster to the basket with the remaining tails of wire, tying them firmly in place.

## YOU WILL NEED

Dried peonies

Dried *Nigella damascena*

Dried gypsophila

Dried pink roses

Secateurs or scissors

Reel wire

Dried lavender

Florist's tape

Paper ribbon

Medium gauge stub wire

## VARIATIONS

If you like this idea, but want to scale it down, try smaller baskets and fill them with little fruits such as grapes, lychees, plums or berries. Instead of wiring on dried flower clusters, stick flower heads and leaves to the basket rim with a glue gun.

**2** Continue to form little flower clusters and wire them around one side of the basket, always securing them so that the flower heads face the same way. Build up the display, covering the wired stems of each cluster with the heads of the next small bunch.

**3** To add depth and contrast to this design, use small bunches of lavender. The deep blue-mauve is the perfect foil to the soft pinks and creams of the other flowers. When you reach the end of one side, neaten the wire by winding some florist's tape over the top.

**4** When you have completed both sides of the basket, make a small cluster of flowers and tape them to the handle (tape is more stable than wire at this point). This gives the design a little continuity. You will cover the tape with the bow, but keep it as neat as you can.

**5** Paper ribbon must be teased apart before it can be used. When you have a sufficient length, fold it into a bow shape and wrap a piece of stub wire around the centre to secure it. Don't cut off the wire tails as these can be used to attach the bow to the handle. Finish off the bow by wrapping a smaller piece of ribbon around the centre to cover the wire. Cut the tails of the bow into deeply angled swallow's tails.

# TABLE DECORATIONS GALLERY

## Leafy cutlery ties

Break away from traditional place settings by tying each guest's cutlery with a trailing stem of fake foliage. You could also adapt this for napkins, too.

## Jewelled napkin rings

Gold *Nigella* seedheads have been cut in half and glued to a napkin ring made from cut cardboard tubes wound with string and painted in purple, silver and gold.

## Miniature iced cakes

A truly lovely gift — you can make one cake for each guest to take home with them. Cut a larger cake into smaller pieces, ice and add iridescent ribbon and frosted violets or scented geranium leaves to decorate.

## Christmas nut star

A glossy addition to the Christmas table: wire is shaped into a star and studded with gold and silver nuts, leaves and cones.

## Pressed flower napkin rings

These napkin rings are made from papier mâché which has been painted with emulsion paint. Pressed flowers and leaves have been glued into place and the ring has been varnished for protection.

## Carnation ties

Fake silk and parchment carnations look almost better than the real thing. Sew them on to check ribbon to create a chic and elegant napkin or cutlery tie.

## Floating flowers

Ever popular, quick to assemble and long-lasting, this table centrepiece shows off the pretty heads of the gerbera to their best advantage. Creamy coloured floating candles complete the display.

# BRIDE'S HEADDRESS

*Whether the bride decides to wear a traditional veil or not, flowers make the perfect headdress. As fresh flowers seldom stand the test of time, or a warmly radiating head, choose silk versions, which are now so enchanting they almost look better than the real thing. Try to buy silk flowers which have been dusted with powder to give them a softer, more authentic appearance.*

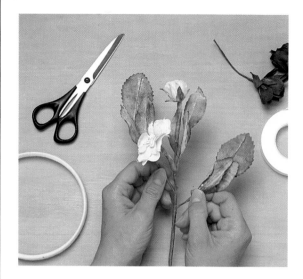

**1** Silk flowers are often sold in clusters, with several flower heads and leaves grouped on one stem. These are easy to pull apart to give you individual flowers and smaller leaf clusters. Use secateurs, strong scissors or wire cutters to trim down the stems.

## YOU WILL NEED

Silk flowers in cream, plum and deep burgundy

Secateurs, strong scissors or wire cutters

White headband

White florist's tape

Pearl clusters

All-purpose glue

*Lapsana* or gypsophila

## TIP

To be really sure that your design is working, fit your headband on to a large doll or wig stand before you begin adding the flowers. Attach the flowers with small bits of sticky tape, which you can lift off and stick down as much as you want until you have a design with which you are happy.

2 Begin to lay the flowers — one or two at a time — against the headband and secure them with tape. Use quite small lengths of tape to secure just two or three stems. Keep the tape as neat as possible; although it is unlikely to show, it should look perfect for that most special day.

3 Work around the band, adding the flowers and leaves in small groupings. Occasionally intersperse a deep coloured flower for contrast. Gently slip the band on to your own head and check your progress. Adjust the floral arrangement accordingly until you are pleased with the result.

4 Pearl clusters are sold in small posies by floral suppliers. Untwist the paper which binds them and separate out into smaller groups. Add these at intervals around the band by pushing them into the tape which is already holding the flowers (add a small dab of glue if you wish).

5 Finally, soften the design with wispy stems of Lapsana or gypsophila. Lapsana is probably the better choice as the flower heads are really tiny and more delicate. Insert these into the headband in the same way that you added the pearls. A small dab of glue is probably advisable here, but avoid using a glue gun which can leave messy, spider's-web trails.

# WEDDING PENDANT

*Weddings are the perfect excuse for spending just a little extra on fresh flowers to create one or a pair of floral pendants. They can be hung at the entrance to a church or, for civil ceremonies, used to decorate the room where the celebrations will be held. A pendant can be made in advance and transported to the venue; however, it is probably much easier to assemble it in situ on the morning of the wedding.*

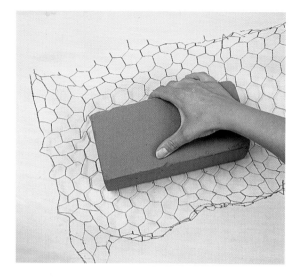

**1** Soak the foam well but ensure it is not dripping. Lay the two pieces of foam on to a rectangle of chicken wire end to end and twist in the wire, securing the sharp ends (wear the gloves for protection). Mould the wire around the foam until you have a long, rectangular shape. Add a heavy gauge piece of wire at the top to serve as a hanging loop (see page 119).

## YOU WILL NEED

2 bricks of fresh florist's foam

Gardening gloves

Chicken wire

Heavy gauge stub wire

Yellow lilies

Cream roses

Pale orange lilies

Deep apricot roses

Eucalyptus foliage

Gypsophila

Exotic seedheads

Emulsion paint (cream) (optional)

Cream paper ribbon

Medium gauge stub wire

## — VARIATIONS —

I've used rich golden yellow and deep apricot, highlighted with cream, but you could try other colour schemes. Pink 'Stargazer' lilies with roses in shades of pink; deep orange lilies offset with orange and peach coloured roses; or cream 'Madonna' lilies with cream and pale yellow tea roses for a purer look would each look equally good.

**2** Turn the shape over and lay on to the worksurface. Now form a loose 'S' shape with the yellow lilies, cutting the stems short and using flower heads that are open and unblemished. (Remember to snip off the stamens first, see page 120 for more details.)

**3** Fill in around the lilies with sprays of cream roses and some of the pale orange lilies. Keep the stems of the lilies short, but the rose stems can be a little longer to form the small sprays. At this stage, it is probably better to hang the pendant in place so that you can assess the display as you work.

**4** Continue to build up the design with sprays of apricot and cream roses, filling in around the sides and base with foliage. To define the shape of the pendant, create a curving spray of apricot-coloured roses at the base.

**5** Tuck in small pieces of the eucalyptus foliage to fill in any gaps, then soften the whole display with clusters of wispy gypsophila. Finally, to add a little interest, wire up a few unusual seedheads (see page 118) and slot these into the arrangement. I dabbed these with a little cream-coloured emulsion paint first to help them blend more harmoniously with the bridal colours. Tie some paper ribbon into a generous bow and attach to the top of the pendant with a piece of stub wire.

# WEDDING FLOWERS GALLERY

### Rose petal confetti (below)
Dried rose petals are possibly the most romantic choice to scatter over the bride and groom. Dry as described on page 116 and add a few drops of rose essential oil to a bag of the petals a week or so before the wedding.

### Silver horseshoe
A traditional gift for the bride which she can carry with her after the ceremony. Decorate a bought silver horseshoe with tiny dried pink rosebuds and gypsophila. Add the narrowest cream silk ribbon.

### Fresh flower boules
A lovely alternative to posies, these flower boules can be carried by bride or bridesmaids alike. Simply stud a soaked foam sphere with chrysanthemum flowerheads and wire in a hanging loop of ribbon.

### Heather buttonhole
An alternative to the traditional buttonhole favoured by men at wedding gatherings. Heather is, of course, the ideal choice for a Scottish (or those with Scottish roots) wedding. Tie with a piece of tartan ribbon.

## Purple buttonhole

Suitable for men or women, this purple buttonhole is made from long-lasting scabious and statice. Tie with a simple cream satin ribbon.

## Wedding corsage

A wedding corsage is very popular and here, creamy alstroemeria are wrapped in white tulle and finished with a satin bow.

## Bridesmaid's hair circlet

Every bridesmaid — particularly the younger ones — long to look like princesses on the wedding day, and this romantic dried and fake flower hair garland is fit for the finest. Florist's wire is twisted into a circlet and covered with fake ivy foliage, cream and pink lace, peonies and deep red rosebuds. Use a glue gun rather than wire.

# PAINTING GLASS

Decorating glassware has been a popular craft for centuries and indeed some of the glass in this book has been inspired by old European work. Now that there are so many excellent products on the market, glass painting is enjoying an enormous revival and every craft magazine on the newsagents' shelves contains yet more ideas and designs.

We have inspired, supported, amused and entertained each other for almost twenty years. On many occasions our children have been reared in the inevitable chaos associated with combining our talents in creative ventures. We both became interested in glass painting when a new product, Porcelaine 150, became available which has very good dishwasher resistance and is safe to use with food — this idea really appealed and has revolutionised the craft. It means that as well as making purely decorative items or ones needing careful hand-washing, everyday glassware may be painted which will stand up to tough washing.

During the past few months we have been busy painting, stencilling, sponging, marbling and etching any and every glass item in our homes, our friends' and parents' homes. Our craving to embellish has included anything from humble jam jars and wine bottles to carafes and glasses, mirrors and even window panes ... nothing has escaped the Lynda and Moira treatment. It has led to our homes being filled with glasses no-one is allowed to drink from in case they dare drop them before this book is printed!

Trips for the weekly food shop have taken on a new appeal. Never mind what the product is, tastes like or costs — what will the bottle look like given a coat of paint? This has led to severe confusion. Just what IS that strange yellow stuff in that jam jar in the fridge? Is it mustard dressing, lemon and honey vinaigrette or custard? And how long does it keep for? If only we had labelled things before parting the mysterious contents from their beautiful containers!

And as for Jim, Lynda's husband — he became increasingly bewildered that the sponge cloth used for washing the dishes was getting smaller by the day (it was a truly marvellous discovery when we found just how good they are for sponging glassware)! All we can say is thank you Jim for putting up with us, our mess, our glass, our experiments and our masterpieces! It has certainly spared Tony, who, as anyone who has read *Dough Craft in a Weekend* will know, has a strong aversion to Moira and her mess!

We have had enormous fun putting together all the ideas in this book and we hope that you will be inspired by them. No particular artistic skill is required as we have described, step-by-step, how to arrive at the finished designs. We have provided templates and patterns where necessary but you will see from the gallery shots just how much stylish glassware can be made with just a few simple brushstrokes and dots of outliner.

Have fun!

*Moira Neal.*

*Lynda Howarth*

Moira and Lynda... partners in design

# GETTING STARTED

*One of the greatest advantages of painting on glass is that the craft requires very little in the way of specialised tools or equipment – just a plentiful supply of new or old glassware which can be picked up for very little money. You will probably discover that much of the equipment listed below can be found around the home. This chapter explains the different paints and demonstrates the basic decorating techniques used in the projects that follow later in the book. Once you have mastered these, you will be able to create a wide range of effects and finishes and adapt them to make your own patterns.*

## EQUIPMENT AND MATERIALS

Your local hobby shop, paint outlet or mail order company will be able to supply the glass paints and other basic materials to get you started. Begin with just a few colours and add to them gradually as your skill and enthusiasm grow. The other equipment you will need to begin is listed in detail in the middle column of this page.

As soon as you have bought your glass paints you will be inspired to make a start. Do not be surprised if your first efforts look very amateurish as it can take a few projects to master this skill. It is therefore a good idea to start off with a really simple design on a jam jar in order to become familiar with the texture of the paint and its application.

It will not be long before you have exhausted your own supply of plain glass and will be requesting friends and relatives to collect empty containers for you too. Everyday packaging suddenly becomes remarkably interesting once the labels are removed and a little imagination is employed!

| |
|---|
| Interesting jars, bottles and glassware |
| Good quality brushes, no 2 and 4 |
| Glass paints according to the project required. Some are solvent-based and suitable for decorative items. For more durability, choose oven-bake water-based paints |
| Outliner in a variety of colours |
| White spirit |
| Jam jar |
| Kitchen paper towels |
| Low-tack masking tape |
| Pencil |
| Scalpel with no 11 blade or craft knife |
| Tracing paper |
| Cocktail sticks (toothpicks) |
| Sponge or fur fabric |
| Cotton buds |
| Cellophane |
| Hairdryer |
| Apron |
| Newspaper, to protect your worksurface |
| Additional useful items for styling your finished work include raffia and florist's wire |

## SOURCING GLASSWARE

If, like us, you are delighted to have an excuse to go to a car boot fair or a jumble or garage sale, glass painting gives you the perfect reason! So much beautiful old glassware is available in an abundance of shapes and sizes at very reasonable prices. Even a batch of dissimilar glasses can be united into a set simply by painting them with the same colour or design motifs.

Look for unusual items such as goldfish bowls, old perfume bottles, engraved glasses, picture frames, clip frames, mirrors and vases.

Make sure you clean your glass very thoroughly before you begin painting. Really stubborn stains inside bottles may be removed with denture cleaner dissolved in hot water. Sticky labels can often be removed by rubbing with a drop of nail varnish remover on a pad of cotton wool.

### TIP

To keep the mess down, once you are ready to begin, protect your workspace with layers of old newspaper or an old tablecloth as some of the paints are solvent-based and may damage some surfaces.

If children are going help with the painting, make sure they are also well covered up.

### SAFETY NOTES

There is no reason why children cannot enjoy the hobby of glass painting as well as adults. Make sure that they are supervised at all times and choose water-based paints for them to use. Store paints and brush cleaner in a cool place, well out of the reach of prying hands when not in use.

Always follow manufacturers' specific instructions regarding the baking process if it is required (see facing page for more details).

mainly transparent and quick drying. Replace the tops to prevent evaporation. Brushes need to be cleaned using a compatible solvent, generally white spirit. These paints are flammable and should not be used near a naked flame nor should children use them unsupervised. Make sure your work area is well ventilated.

### SAFETY NOTE

Please refer to manufacturer's specific user and safety instructions regarding all glass paints. As a general rule, never paint any surface which is to come into contact with food unless the paint is non-toxic (this is why we decorated the backs of the plates) and as an extra precaution, avoid the lip line on glasses which are going to be functional and not simply used as decorations.

A collection of glassware ready for painting

# GLASS PAINTING PRODUCTS

There are many paints available on the market for painting on glass. They tend to fall into several categories:

1 Water-based paints. These do not need baking and are ideal for items which will not require washing. These are perfect for children to use too.

2 Water-based paints. These need to be baked at 200°C/400°F/gas mark 6 for 30 minutes. Items using this paint are hand-washable. The colours are bright and dense and easy to apply.

3 Porcelaine 150, Pébéo's water-based paints. These are baked at 150°C/300°F/gas mark 2. These are completely safe when in contact with food and have good dishwasher resistance. These are ideal for tableware and glasses and we have used them extensively in this book. They are available in a huge range of colours, both transparent

and opaque, and once baked feel wonderfully smooth. Practice may be needed with these, as indeed with all paints, to achieve the density of cover required. It is often better to sponge on two light coats, allowing the first to dry before applying the second. There is a matt medium in the range which, if used alone, gives a wonderful, frosted effect. Used with the other colours in the range as instructed, it gives a matt finish without affecting the colour.

4 Pébéo's water-based gel paints. A new product on the market is a water-based gel which allows three-dimensional colour to be applied to glassware direct from the tube or with the aid of a palette knife. Glass nuggets, tiny mirrors and other items may then be embedded in the gel before it sets for an exotic effect. This enables you to imitate various blown glass effects, as well as creating stylish jewellery. Available in a range of colours, the gel liquifies when shaken or stirred so may also be applied with a brush.

5 Solvent-based paints. These tend to be the paints associated with the traditional stained glass look and are

# OUTLINING

The outliners used in this book are water-based, although there are some which become permanent with baking. They can be difficult to control, so practise on jam jars or cellophane before embarking on the real thing.

Have a sheet of kitchen paper ready to catch any blobs of outliner from the tube which may appear as soon as the top is removed. Start by making a row of dots and you will soon realise how little pressure is required on the tube. Progress to circles, squares, triangles and lines ①. You may find you get a halo effect at times — do not worry as this

can be salvaged once the outliner has dried and can be eased back into place with the scalpel. A hairdryer is useful for speeding up the drying times of both outliners and paints but needs to be kept at least 15 cm (6 in) away from the surface to avoid damage.

## USING THE GLASS PAINTS

Within about five minutes the outliner will be dry enough to apply the paint. A soft brush is essential for smooth application of the paints ①. Try filling in some of the shapes you have made with the outliners. Apply the paint with even strokes. Keep a cotton bud nearby to correct any errors and a small jar of water or solvent for brush cleaning.

## SPONGING

Sponging gives a soft, delicate effect and is a very quick and easy way to apply glass paints.

Tip a few drops of the paint into a saucer (covered with cling film to reduce the cleaning up). Gently dip in your sponge pad and wipe any excess off against the edge of the dish and then test the effect on a piece of cellophane or an old jam jar before starting on your project.

One colour can be used on its own to produce a graded effect just by applying more paint onto the lowest part of the item, reducing the pressure and contact as you move up ②. A graduated effect is achieved by using several colours in succession, allowing each one to merge into the next ③.

---

### TIP

Thin sponge dishcloths are ideal for glass painting as they can be cut up into small pieces and discarded after use. Fine fur fabric also produces an even sponged finish but the rough edges should be folded in before use to prevent any fibres migrating onto the surface of the glass.

## SPONGE DOT APPLICATORS

A really simple way to apply uniform dots to a project is to make your own applicators. Peel a foam dishcloth into two and then cut it into 2 cm (¾ in) squares. Bind each one over the end of a cocktail stick or toothpick using fuse wire. Make several as you will find them a useful addition to your equipment kit!

## STENCILLING

This is a good way to decorate glassware with a regular repeat pattern. It is particularly useful if you intend to sell your finished items as it is very quick to do once the initial stencil cutting has been done.

To make your stencils, photocopy the required template (see page 185), use adhesive mount to attach it to the card you are using and allow the glue to dry for about ten minutes before attempting to cut it. Protect your worksurface with a cutting mat, cork mat or a thick layer of newspaper before you start. Use a metal ruler as a guide for cutting straight lines ①. Avoid trying to cut around angular designs in one go; instead, make several shorter cuts ②.

It is worth taking care in order to get good, professional results and the initial investment in a craft knife or scalpel and plenty of spare blades is worthwhile. For one-off stencils to decorate flat surfaces, thin card is ideal or even a good quality paper. If you are using your stencil on a curved surface, you may need to use either thin paper or specialist adhesive stencilling film which moulds more easily to the contours of the glass.

## USING STENCILS

Lightly spray the back of the stencil with aerosol glue and press it onto the object to be decorated. On cylindrical items you may also need to secure the stencil with a couple of rubber bands.

③ Pour a little glass paint into a saucer and use either a piece of old

❶

❷

❸

reinforcements or indeed any shape you care to cut out of paper.

Use aerosol adhesive mount to apply your own shapes to the glass. Masking tape, torn strips of newspaper and very thin tape available from art shops can also be used. Squares, oblongs, stripes of varying widths and harlequin designs are all possible this way, producing very effective results ①, ②.

It is so easy to produce fabulous glassware with minimal artistic ability using these ideas. If you wish, the masked off area can later be embellished with outliner to add a relief pattern, such as the veining on a leaf. This method can also be used to add a regular pattern, for example to the outer edge of a plate.

Simple, Shaker-style stencil, ideal for beginners

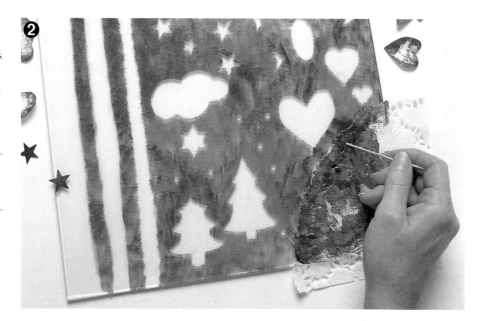

sponge or fur fabric to apply the paint. It is always worth experimenting at this stage and we found that fur fabric works wonderfully well for a fine, even texture. Sponge will give a rougher, less even texture which is more suitable for rustic style projects ④.

## MASKING AND REVERSE STENCILLING

Many different objects can be used to mask out clear areas on the glass before you decorate with sponging or marbling. Stick on shapes like stars, hearts, flowers, initials, ring

# ETCHING

This is a very good way to add embellishment without having to use another colour. It is perfect for adding details like feathers, scales on fish, eyes and so on as well as creating abstract designs on a sponged surface. You will need to etch the design as soon as the paint has been applied and there are several ways of doing it. Use a cocktail stick or toothpick for very fine designs or for details on tiny items. A typist's 'pencil' type of rubber is ideal for chunkier etching and may be sharpened with a knife or pencil sharpener depending on the effect required ①. Knitting needles work well too.

# MARBLING

A wonderful range of patterns may be produced using this technique which involves floating coloured solvent-based glass paints on a suitable medium. We have kept the procedure simple and have avoided the use of specialist marbling mediums in preference for water and wallpaper paste. You will need to use a bowl larger than the size of the item to be marbled and cover the worksurface with plenty of paper before you begin.

One of the projects in this book has marbling as one of the stages of producing the final item. Refer to page 154 for fuller instructions.

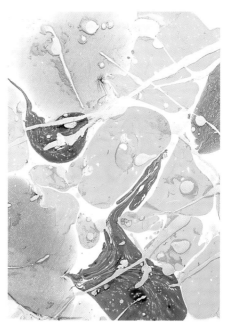

Sponged and etched snowflake plate

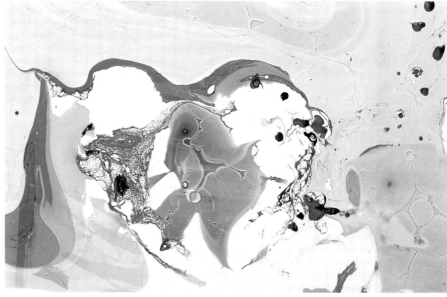

An exotic effect created by marbling a simple piece of glass

## TRANSFERRING DESIGNS

The easiest way to transfer a design onto glass is to trace it. Tape the design to the inside or back of the object to hold it firmly against the glass. If the surface is curved, make many small vertical slits to enable the pattern to conform to the glass. Trace over the pattern with outliner.

## NARROW NECKED BOTTLES

It is impossible to tape the design to the inside of narrow necked bottles but there is a simple solution. Make sure the bottle is dry inside and then, on a piece of paper, cut out the design to the height of the bottle. Roll up the paper, push it into the bottle, then pour in pasta or lentils right up to the top and the design is perfectly anchored! ①

❷

❶

## EMBELLISHMENTS

The addition of those lovely shiny glass nuggets available in a myriad of colours gives a very splendid finish to an otherwise ordinary item. Tiny rhinestones and sequins may be used too and they are available from craft shops or mail order companies ②.

Apply them to your glassware before the paint using a specialist glass glue to

## REVERSE PAINTING TECHNIQUE

This is a very handy way to decorate the back of a glass plate so that the cutting surface will not become damaged when the plate is used. It is also useful if you wish to use paints which are not safe when in contact with food. A little planning is needed before you begin because the details, normally left until last, must be painted on first. Just think in reverse and remember to reverse any text too!

These iridescent nuggets inspired this floral design

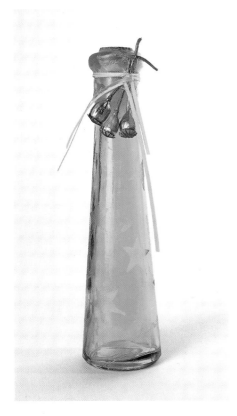

Matt medium was applied over a star stencil for this subtle effect

ensure good adhesion. If you are giving a filled, decorated bottle to a friend as a present, spend some time adding a label, a pretty stopper or sealing wax. See our gallery pages for more ideas. Remember, a beautifully presented item will quickly lead to orders if you want to sell your glassware.

# INSPIRATION FOR DESIGNS

Wrapping paper, gift cards, colouring books, curtain fabrics, flower and bulb catalogues are good sources of inspiration. Do remember, however, that you may not sell any work using other people's designs.

For a baby gift you could use the nursery wallpaper design to inspire the edge of a mirror or picture frame. Glasses, jugs and carafes decorated to match existing crockery or table linen make excellent gifts for adults and may be themed to celebrate a special occasion, such as a milestone birthday or anniversary.

If you enjoy museums, why not visit one and get inspiration from old

European glassware? We found some fascinating pieces where much of the design is made up of dots and swirls — very easy to reproduce as you can see from the bottle above.

This design was adapted from traditional East European glassware

# GOLDFISH PLATE

*A shoal of golden fish swim around this plate which is both practical and attractive. You could use it to brighten up your bathroom, and could decorate other items such as a soap dish or toothbrush mug to match. As the plate is decorated on the underside, it may be used for serving food.*

**1** Wash the plate in hot soapy water and dry carefully. Start by sponging the edge of the plate on the underside with the gold paint, applying it densely around the outside. Allow the paint to look feathery on the inner edge. Use the paper towel and white spirit to clean any paint from the front of the plate.

## VARIATIONS

This plate could be painted using oven-bake paints if you want to preserve the pattern during frequent use. It seems a pity to hide it away in a cupboard when not in use, so why not store it on a plate display stand?

**2** Copy the large fish template and tape it to the inside of the plate, positioning it centrally. Working on the back of the plate, paint the fish gold, but do not apply the markings at this stage.

**3** Remove the template and use it as a guide to etch in the details of the scales and gills using the cocktail stick. Keep the tip clean with the paper towel.

**4** Paint the shoal of tiny goldfish next. This time have a practise run on cellophane first as it is easier to copy the tiny shapes we have given you. Use the cocktail stick to etch in the details after every third or fourth fish. For a bit of fun, paint one little fish swimming the wrong way! Allow the plate to dry for about an hour while you make the surf template for the next stage.

**5** Draw around the plate onto a piece of paper. Cut out the circle and then fold it in half four times to make 16 equal sections. Open it out flat and mark 1 cm (½ in) in from the edge all the way round. Trace the surf template onto each marked section. Pour some of the white paint onto the saucer, dip the sponge into it and wipe the excess off on the edge. Sponge the surf design all around the plate. Remove the template and quickly soften the edges of the wave design by carefully sponging over it. Turn the plate over every now and then to check what it looks like from the front. Leave the plate upside down to dry for 24 hours before use.

# FAUX TORTOISESHELL PLATE

*This plate was inspired by the fascinating shapes and colours of natural tortoiseshell. Why not do as we have and create a complete set of matching glassware using different sized bottles and pots? A combination of painting and marbling was used and we can guarantee that you will end up with a totally unique piece each time!*

**1** Wash and dry the plate before you begin in order to remove any grease. Paint the back of the plate with the yellow paint using long brushstrokes. Do not try to get this too even as imperfections will add to the natural look of the plate. Leave it to dry or speed up the process with a hairdryer.

## VARIATIONS

Why stick to traditional tortoiseshell colours? As long as the base colour is pale and will tone with the two marbled coats, all kinds of variations are possible. It is worth experimenting on cellophane before you reach a decision as it is much simpler to throw it out than it is to clean a plate!

2 Fill the bowl with water and then fill the pipettes with both the brown paints. Quickly drop the paint on the surface of the water and allow the drops to merge slightly. Position the plate over the marbled surface and 'roll' the plate away from you picking up the marbled pattern on the back of the plate (see step 4 below). Place the plate upside down to dry.

3 For the second marbling, a more spattered effect is achieved by squirting the paints over the water so that it breaks up into smaller drops. Any unsightly blobs may be carefully removed using a cocktail stick to roll the paint off the surface of the water.

4 Again, lower the plate onto the marbled surface as indicated in step 2, above. Leave the plate upside down to dry once more. You can use a hairdryer to speed up the drying process, if you wish.

5 Touch up any imperfections using a fine brush and the yellow basecoat and leave to dry for at least 24 hours before use. For extra scratch resistance, the back may be painted with two coats of polyurethane varnish.

# YELLOW GALLERY

**'Volcano' oil burner**
This has been etched and over-painted.

**Tall yellow bottle**
This elegant bottle has been stencil-frosted for a pretty finish.

**Orange slices jar**
A citrus effect was achieved by applying the paint with a very small brush and fine brushstrokes.

**Shallow yellow platter**
A very simple gold border was painted around this dish for a striking effect.

**Cup and saucer**
Luscious apricots were painted on this cup using opaque glass paints.

**Shaped glasses**
One glass has been painted with simple bands of yellow and gold and the other given an iridescent effect by being lightly sponged first with gold and then with a clear yellow. A simple band of gold dots was added later.

## 1940s' style glass dessert dish

*Bottom:* The embossed lines on this dish made it very simple to decorate with yellows, orange and gold.

## Perfume bottle

Matt medium was used on this little bottle first and then the yellow paint applied, making the glass appear transparent again.

## Hexagonal jar

*Bottom:* Low-tack tape was used to mask off alternate facets before marbling with yellow, orange and gold. Gold outliner dots were added later.

## Tall, pale yellow glass

The bowl of this glass was made from pale lemon glass but a deeper colour was overlaid using clear yellow paint.

## Copper glass

This glass was frosted with matt medium first before a coat of copper was sponged over the bottom section.

## Stripy frosted glass

Strips of paper were used to mask off areas and matt medium then sponged on to give a frosted look.

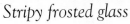

# STAINED GLASS MIRROR

*The colour selection of red, blue and green has made this simple mirror look quite exotic! The outline shapes could also be used as a solid design to decorate a wine bottle or jam jars with great success. It is easy enough for children to be able to imitate as long as they are carefully supervised, and a myriad of effects can be obtained depending on the colour selection used and the size of each shape.*

**1** Use glass cleaner to remove all traces of grease from the mirror before you begin. Cut the carbon paper to the size of the mirror and lay it face down onto it. Make a copy of the template, enlarging or reducing it as required and lay it over the carbon. Tape it in place. Use the coloured pencil to copy the outline onto the mirror so that you can see what you have already traced.

## YOU WILL NEED

| |
|---|
| Mirror 23 x 18 cm (9 x 7 in) |
| Glass cleaner |
| Carbon paper |
| Scissors |
| Template (page 184) |
| Sticky tape |
| Sharp coloured pencil |
| Paper for protecting your work top |
| Solvent-based paints such as Vitrail in ruby red, blue and green |
| No 2 brush |
| White spirit for brush cleaning |
| Hairdryer (optional) |
| Lead effect outliner |
| Kitchen paper towels |
| Scalpel |

---

### TIP

The beauty of this project is that precision is unimportant so do not worry too much when you are copying the outlines! You may want to have more or less of the mirror showing than we have and it is easy to adjust this in step 1 by altering the size of the template using a photocopier.

**2** Now the fun begins. Load the paintbrush with red paint and allow it to flow onto the mirror. Apply the paint quite thickly to produce a rich colourful effect. Paint about a quarter of the shapes this way. Clean the brush with the white spirit and allow the red areas to dry before using the next colour. This may be speeded up with the use of a hairdryer if you wish.

**3** Apply the green to a further quarter of the shapes. It does not matter if the edges of your painted areas are uneven as the outliner will hide a multitude of sins!

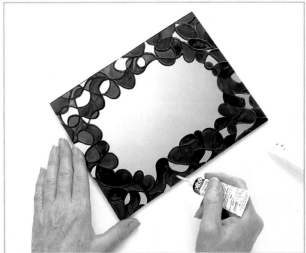

**4** Finally, use blue glass paint to fill in all but a quarter of the shapes. These remaining plain mirrored spaces can be embellished with the addition of rhinestones, glass nuggets or sequins, securing them in place with glass glue, or left plain as we have done.

**5** Now use the outliner to trace over the pencil line in the mirror. Apply even pressure to the tube and have a paper towel to hand to keep the nozzle clean Finally, edge the mirror with the outliner to give a finished look. Allow the mirror to dry for about 24 hours before use, and polish off any fingerprints.

# STARRY OIL BURNER

*These beautiful, simple glass burners are perfect for decorating with glass paints and can be painted, etched or sponged to suit any occasion. They are available in several different shapes and sizes and are economic to run. No more dripping candle wax! Make sure you use oven-bake paints to prevent any lamp oil coming into contact with the surface and dissolving your creation.*

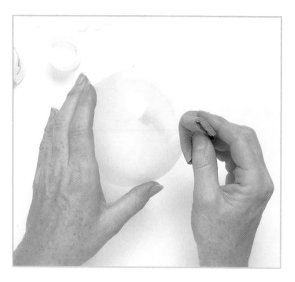

**1** Remove the wick and holder from the burner and plug the hole with adhesive putty. Wash the burner in hot, soapy water and dry thoroughly. Sponge the matt medium over the entire surface. Put some of the matt medium on the jam jar too as it will be useful in step 5. The paint looks transparent when it is first applied but it dries quickly. When dry, apply a second coat. A hairdryer will speed up the process.

### YOU WILL NEED

Round glass oil burner

Jam jar

Re-usable adhesive putty

Small piece of sponge

Oven-bake paints such as Porcelaine 150 in pewter and matt medium

Porcelaine 150 pewter outliner

No 2 paintbrush

Water

Hairdryer (optional)

Large and small star templates (page 185)

Metal ruler

Scalpel with a 11 blade

Cutting mat

Pencil

Paper towels

Domestic oven

### SAFETY NOTE

Always follow the manufacturer's instructions supplied with the lamp and never leave it unattended at any time, particularly if you have children or cats in the house.

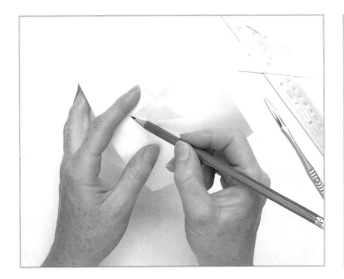

**2** Cut out the star templates using a metal ruler, cutting mat and scalpel. (Refer to the techniques section.) Use the pencil to draw the star outline onto the globe using the photograph as a guide for the spacing. Keep the motifs equidistant.

**3** Paint the marked stars using the pewter paint. The matt base coat is a wonderful surface to paint over. For a really good cover, a second coat is needed.

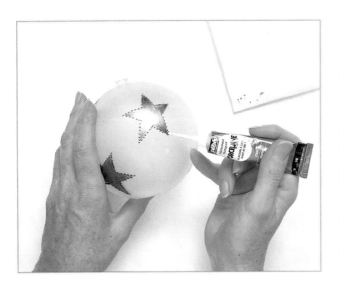

**4** Use the outliner to make rows of tiny dots round each star. Be careful to use the outliner sparingly as it continues to spread. Allow the globe to dry thoroughly before moving on to the next step.

**5** The tiny stars are etched out using the scalpel and the template pattern provided. It is a good idea to practise on the jam jar first before starting on the real thing. Leave the globe to dry for 24 hours before baking following manufacturer's instructions. Once the globe is completely cool, fill it with lamp oil using a tiny funnel to avoid any getting onto the matt surface. Replace the wick in the bottle and light.

## VARIATIONS

Use different coloured lamp oils to make the burner look festive or spring-like. It will look wonderful as a table decoration surrounded with ivy but make sure leaves are kept well away from the flame.

# BLACK, SILVER AND GOLD GALLERY

### Etched cork-stoppered jar
*Bottom:* This jar was frosted with matt medium with the design etched out afterwards.

### Oak and acorn glass
*Bottom:* This design was stencilled on and the detail etched out with a cocktail stick.

### Jug
*Bottom:* As simple as ABC! Letters were drawn on the jug and black dots added around the top.

### Black plate
These stunning white brushstrokes look very oriental but are, in fact, simple random strokes.

### Cocktail glass
Two coats of gold on the outside of this glass were followed by random black spots for a stylish finish.

### Marbled plate
Here black, white and gold paints were floated on water and the design picked up on the back of the plate.

### Frosted carafe
Oak leaves have been stencilled on this carafe using matt medium.

## Art Deco jar

*Bottom*: This jar has been decorated very simply with stylised deer.

## Glasses

*Below*: It is so easy to unite several dissimilar glasses like these with a common colour scheme. Black, gold and white paints and outliners were used to apply the designs.

## Christmas bauble

Not even the humble bauble can escape decoration! This one was patterned with outliner.

## Art Deco perfume bottle

*Centre*: This bottle was sponged with silver and gold before the stylised design was added in black.

## Black and white dappled plate

Blobs of black and white paint were dropped onto the back of the plate and then spread and etched with a cocktail stick.

## Perfume bottle

*Bottom*: This bottle embellished with trefoils was decorated with the pattern on page 184.

## Gold and black glass

This glass was made in the same way as the set of decorated glasses on pages 164 – 165.

# DECORATED WINE GLASSES

*Here is a really clever way to decorate glasses and a matching carafe simply with the help of a few rubber bands. Use this technique to mask off sections which are then sponged in one colour. Neat rows of dots add a finishing touch. The perfect project for the non-artistic!*

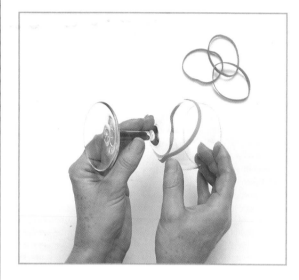

**1** Wash all the items in hot soapy water and dry thoroughly. Place a rubber band around the glass 1 cm (½ in) from the top on one side to the same distance from the stem at the bottom. Take time to adjust the band evenly for best results. The width of the band will determine the space between the coloured areas; the band measurement given is the minimum you should use. It is advisable to avoid the lip line if using a paint other than that specified.

## YOU WILL NEED

Set of glasses and carafe

Jam jar for practice runs

3 x 5 mm (¼ in) rubber bands for each item to be decorated

Porcelaine 150 glass paints in your choice of opaque colours

Porcelaine 150 outliner

Small piece of fur fabric or fine sponge for each colour being used

Saucer covered in cling film to speed the cleaning up process

Scalpel

Domestic oven

## —— VARIATIONS ——

Add a matching carafe to the set using a different colour in each section to unite it with the glasses. Experiment with different colour combinations and outliners. This idea can be adapted to make little candle holders decorated with solvent-based paints to give a stained glass effect.

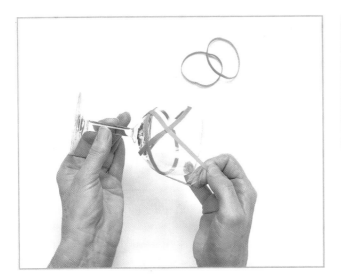

2 Repeat with the second and third rubber bands aiming to spread them equally around the bowl of the glass so that all the sections to be painted are roughly the same size. If you are planning to decorate a carafe to match the set, add bands to it as well.

3 Pour a little paint into the saucer and then sponge the spaces between the bands with your chosen colour. Apply the colour lightly and evenly for best results. We painted all six areas the same colour on each glass but you could use six different colours. Paint the stems too, as we have, or leave them plain. Leave for 24 hours to dry before being tempted to go on to step 4!

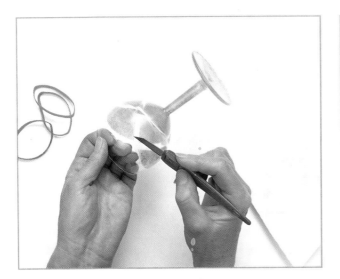

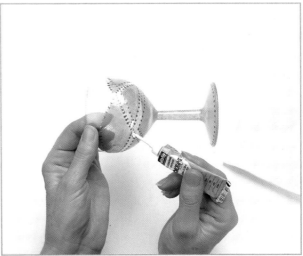

4 Remove the bands and you will find that the paint has seeped under the rubber where they cross. Use a scalpel to neaten up the edges.

5 Using the outliner, apply tiny dots around each block of colour to give a really neat finish. Remember that the outliner tends to spread slightly so leave space between each dot. (It might be worth practising first on a jam jar.) If you are happy with the result, leave for a further 24 hours before baking following manufacturer's instructions. If not, wash the design off and start again! Wash the glasses before use.

# FROSTED GLASS WINDOW

*Here is a cheap but attractive alternative to frosted glass. It is also a good substitute for net curtaining at windows where you need a little extra privacy. The painting may be done on the inside of an existing window if self-curing paint is used, or on a sheet of glass cut to size as we have done, in which case oven-bake paints may be used for scratch resistance. Use a photocopier to enlarge or reduce the pattern to suit any size of window.*

**1** Enlarge the pattern using a photocopier to the size required if necessary. Use aerosol mount to attach it to the thin card (if using). Leave to dry for at least ten minutes before cutting the stencil. Place the pattern onto the cutting mat and use the scalpel to cut out the design carefully. Keep the cockerel for step 3.

## VARIATIONS

If you omit the cockerel, this design would look good as a frame for a mirror. With the addition of a few more squares, the pattern can easily be elongated and a row of cockerels added!

2 Thoroughly clean the glass with warm soapy water or glass cleaner and make sure it is completely dry before sponging. Lay the glass onto a piece of coloured paper or fabric so that you can see what you are doing. Use a light spray of adhesive mount on the back of the stencil, leave to dry for a few seconds and then position it centrally on the glass.

3 Pour some opaque white paint into the saucer and use the sponge or fur fabric to apply the paint evenly over the outer design. Hold the glass up to the light to check for even density. Sponge the cockerel last and then remove the stencil with great care and admire before quickly moving on to the next stage!

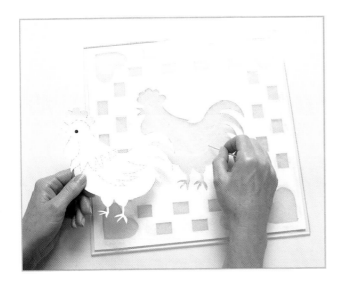

4 Use the typist's rubber or cocktail stick to etch in the eye, wing and other details of the cockerel using the template as a guide.

5 Finally, remove any stray paint which has managed to work its way under the stencil using a cotton bud and then leave to dry for at least 24 hours. Alternatively, use a scalpel to remove the paint once it is completely dry. Bake if appropriate.

TIP

If using oven-bake paints, remember to use a
pane of glass which will fit inside the oven.

# TEXTURED FRUIT TUMBLERS

*There is no need for a template when the design is embossed in the glass as it is in these tumblers. This makes it ideal as a beginner's project. The tumblers are made from recycled glass and similar glassware is widely available. Use the idea on embossed jugs and wine bottles too, and choose jewel-like colours to produce a luscious look.*

**1** Thoroughly wash and dry the glasses in hot soapy water to remove any trace of grease and then dry them in a cool oven. Choose the colours you want to use and test them on a sheet of cellophane before starting on the glassware. Start by painting the lemons and orange slices with the yellow paint.

## YOU WILL NEED

Embossed glasses

Porcelaine 150 glass paints in orange, pink, purple, yellow and green

Cellophane

No 2 paintbrush

Water

Kitchen paper towels

Domestic oven

---

**TIP**

You can easily unite a collection of mismatched textured glassware by painting it in the same colours.

2 Using the orange paint, highlight the citrus slices to give them depth and a rich, fruity look. You may wish to build up colours by using two or more coats of paint.

3 We have chosen a cerise pink for these cherries but if you prefer a brighter look, use a strong red or even a really dark mix of purple and red paint to imitate juicy black cherries.

4 The grapes are painted using the purple. Do not worry if the paint does not lie flat on the surface of the grapes as the nature of the paint is such that it has an uneven effect. In this project this is of benefit as it reflects the natural bloom of the fruit.

5 Finally, paint the foliage green. Leave the tumblers to dry for 24 hours and then bake according to manufacturer's instructions. Wash the glasses before use.

# TURQUOISE GALLERY

### Stoppered bottle

White lilies have been painted on this bottle with silver used for the stamens. Look through flower catalogues for similar ideas.

### Tall turquoise vase

Gold outliner has been applied to give a 'punched' look in simple spirals and curves.

### Floral jar

Bottom: Green and silver paints were used to brighten up this jam jar. A little white was added to the silver for the outer parts of the petals and the white dots of paint applied last.

### Goldfish jar

Below: This would be fun to fill with bubble bath as a gift for a child. The fish were painted with outliner first and then with a coat of clear yellow glass paint.

### Fish platter

Gold was lightly brushed on the back of this plate and then a variety of blues, greens and turquoises painted over it.

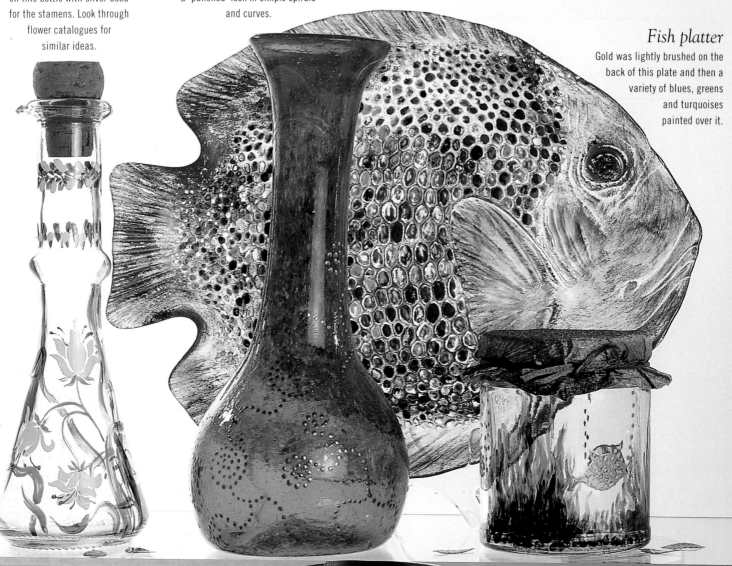

## Two-tone glass

*Bottom*: Transparent oven-bake paints in green and blue were sponged onto this little glass to give a graduated effect.

## Multi-faceted jug

This old jug was picked up at a junk shop and transformed by being sponged with a range of oven-bake paints. Pewter outliner was then dotted around each colour.

## Marbled plate

The edge of the plate was painted with gold and allowed to dry before turquoise, green, purple and gold paints were floated on water, and the plate marbled with them.

## Cup and saucer

*Below*: Just imagine sipping fruit tea from this cup, beautifully painted with blackcurrants. Why not make a set featuring a variety of fruits?

## Tall vase

Simple brushstrokes in shades of blues, greens and gold make this a very quick and easy project.

## Turquoise tumbler

*Left*: The black lines were applied first and then green, white and gold paints to fill some of the spaces.

## Clip frame

Black outliner was allowed to trail in wiggly lines around the frame. Once it was dry, some of the spaces were filled with green, gold and purple paints.

## Encrusted bottle

Chunky glass nuggets were first glued in place on this bottle and the design worked around them.

# FLORAL ROUNDELS

*These roundels make a refreshing change from the usual stained glass versions that are now seen everywhere. They are a perfect way to brighten up a window and look attractive when the sunlight shines through them.*

**1** If your roundel is not the same size as ours, use a photocopier to enlarge or reduce the template to the required dimmensions. Lay the template on the worksurface and tape the roundel over it, being careful to position the tape over plain areas of the pattern.

## VARIATIONS

These designs could be used as jam pot covers if the designs were worked on cellophane using black paint instead of outliner. Enlarge or reduce the design according to the size of the jar and use white tissue underneath it to show off the design.

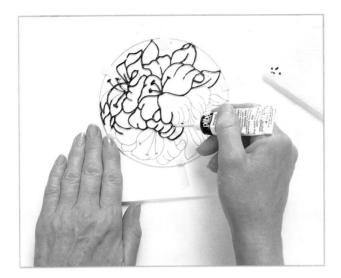

**2** With the outliner, carefully follow the outlines of the flowers and leaves using steady, even pressure. Start at the top and work towards yourself to avoid smudging. Keep a paper towel to hand to remove any blobs of outliner from the tip of the nozzle. Leave to dry or speed up the process with the hairdryer.

**3** If there are any imperfections in the outlining they can be salvaged at this stage. Use a scalpel to scratch off any rough areas and use the paintbrush to gently brush loosened outliner away from the surface.

**4** Practise your brush strokes on cellophane using the ruby paint. Once you are confident, start working on the flowers and brush the petals from the centre outwards to obtain light, feathery strokes.

**5** Finally, paint the leaves with the green paint varying the density of the paint for a more realistic effect and to build up depth.

# RED GALLERY

## Sundae dish

*Below*: The top part of the dish was sponged with red, while gold was used for the lower part. Once dry, tiny spots of gold outliner were added as a decorative pattern.

## Fleur de lys jar

*Bottom left*: Flat-sided jam jars are ideal for decorating. This one was sponged first and then the design added with gold outliner.

## Triangular red bottle

*Bottom*: Sponging forms the basis of the pattern on both these bottles. Outliner has been used for the relief patterns.

## Valentine platter

Simple and sweet for the one you love!

## Faceted jar

This design was inspired by old glassware and could be used very effectively in a range of colours on a set of sundae dishes or tumblers.

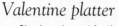

## Octagonal dish

Positive and negative stencilling has been used to decorate this dish with heart motifs.

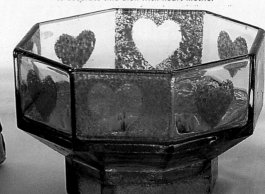

## Bow glass

The bottom part of this glass was sponged with gold. Once dry, the bow motif was stencilled on. You could cut your own stencil or use a commercial one.

## Heart-shaped crown bottle

*Bottom*: Coloured glass bottles are widely available and are easy to decorate. This one features simple but effective designs.

## Spotty bottle

Mineral drinks come in a superb range of shapes and sizes and are ideal for revamping and re-using.

## Strawberry cup

*Bottom*: You do need some artistic skill to reproduce this design, but it could be simplified or even stencilled. Why not paint a set of glass cups with a selection of fruits and use them to serve fruit teas?

## Faceted jug

This wonderful old jug was found at a local junk shop. It lends itself to this kind of decoration and similar pieces of glass are easy to find. A combination of painting and relief work has been used.

# ACKNOWLEDGMENTS

The authors and publishers would like to thank the following companies and organisations:

*Dough Craft*

Thanks to Daler-Rowney for supplying artist's materials, and Lakeland Plastics and Bostic for their assistance.

*Painting Glass*

A very big thank you to Pébéo, in particular John Wright of Pébéo UK and Carol Hook from Clear Communications Ltd, who have been so generous in their supply of paints, especially Porcelaine 150 and Vitrail, which we have used almost exclusively in this book.

Thank you to Clearcraft for their beautiful glass oil burners and to the Egyptian House who generously supplied us with a selection of their lovely coloured and recycled glass. Thank you to the Cambridge branch of Emmaus, the self-help group for the homeless, for having such an abundance of glassware at incredibly good prices just crying out to be painted (we hope there is a branch near you).

*Flower Crafts*

Ascalon Design Parchment Flowers, The Coach House, Aylesmore Court, St Briavels, Gloucestershire GL15 6UQ (01594 530567) who supply a vast range of fabulous parchment flowers and who kindly supplied us the beautiful peony roses on page 124 and sunflower on page 129.

Prices Patent Candle Co Ltd, 110 York Road, London SW11 3RU (0171 228 2001) for the various candles used on page 130.

# STAMPING TEMPLATES

Lino stamps have been used in various projects throughout the book. To make your own lino prints like these, use a photocopier to enlarge or reduce the images as required. Place a piece of carbon paper, ink side down, on to a piece of lino and then place the photocopied image on top of the carbon paper. Trace over the photocopied image and through the carbon paper with a pen or pencil. Remove the carbon paper and photocopied image to reveal a carbon copy of your image. Using a pen go over the image on the lino to give a clearer idea of where to cut. Take a lino cutting tool and carefully cut out the image on the lino. Follow instructions for making a stamp on page 13.

### Hallowe'en Frieze
(see page 28)

### Festive Napkin Holder
(see page 32)

### Wooden Fruit Bowl
(see page 26)

### Flower
(see page 13)

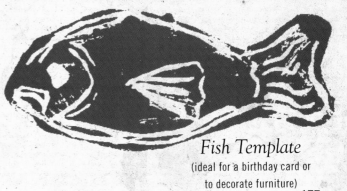

### Fish Template
(ideal for a birthday card or to decorate furniture)

Picture Frame
(see page 23)

Moon Design
(see page 14)

Wooden Chair with Bird
(see page 18)

Mackintosh Rose
(see page 33)

Hallowe'en Frieze
(see page 28)

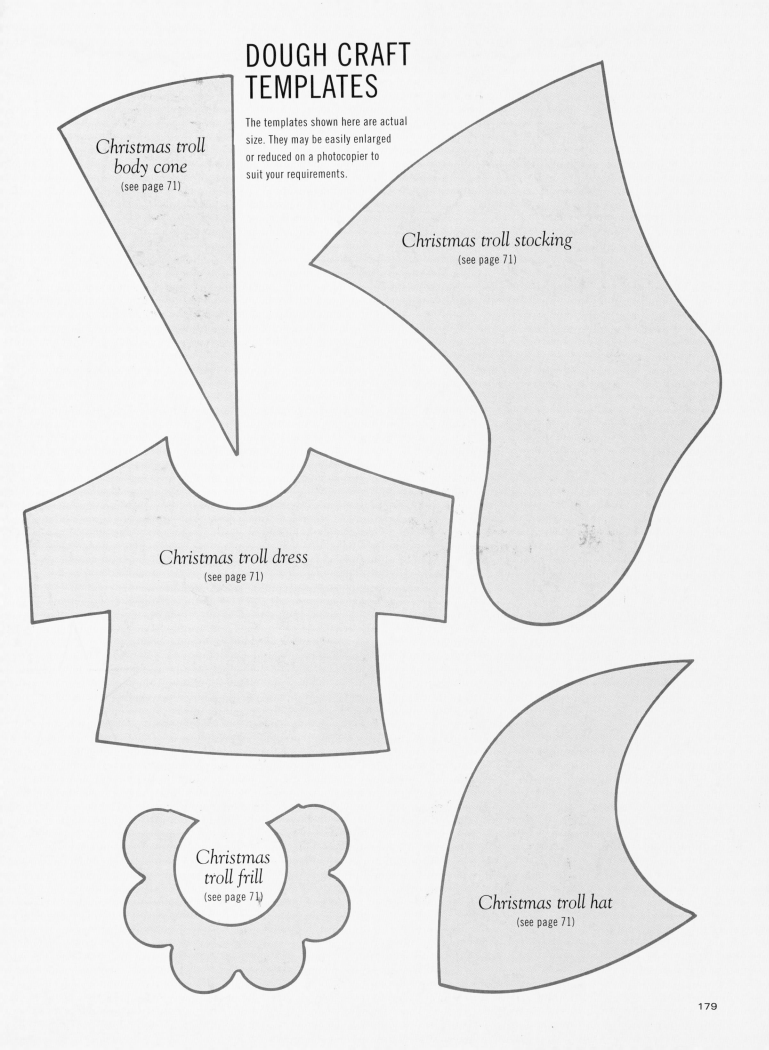

# DOUGH CRAFT TEMPLATES

The templates shown here are actual size. They may be easily enlarged or reduced on a photocopier to suit your requirements.

*Christmas troll body cone*
(see page 71)

*Christmas troll stocking*
(see page 71)

*Christmas troll dress*
(see page 71)

*Christmas troll frill*
(see page 71)

*Christmas troll hat*
(see page 71)

Oak
Leaves
(see page 56)

Apple
Blossom
(see page 48, 54)

Calyxes
(see page 72)

Ivy
Leaves
(see page 50, 54)

Primrose
(see page 54)

Briar
Rose Petals
(see page 70)

Leaves
(see page 48, 56,
70, 72)

Holly Leaves
(see page 69)

Christmas heart
(see page 70)

Small heart
(see page 70)

Star
(see page 70)

Grape
Leaves
(see page 50)

Seaweed
Fronds
(see page 60)

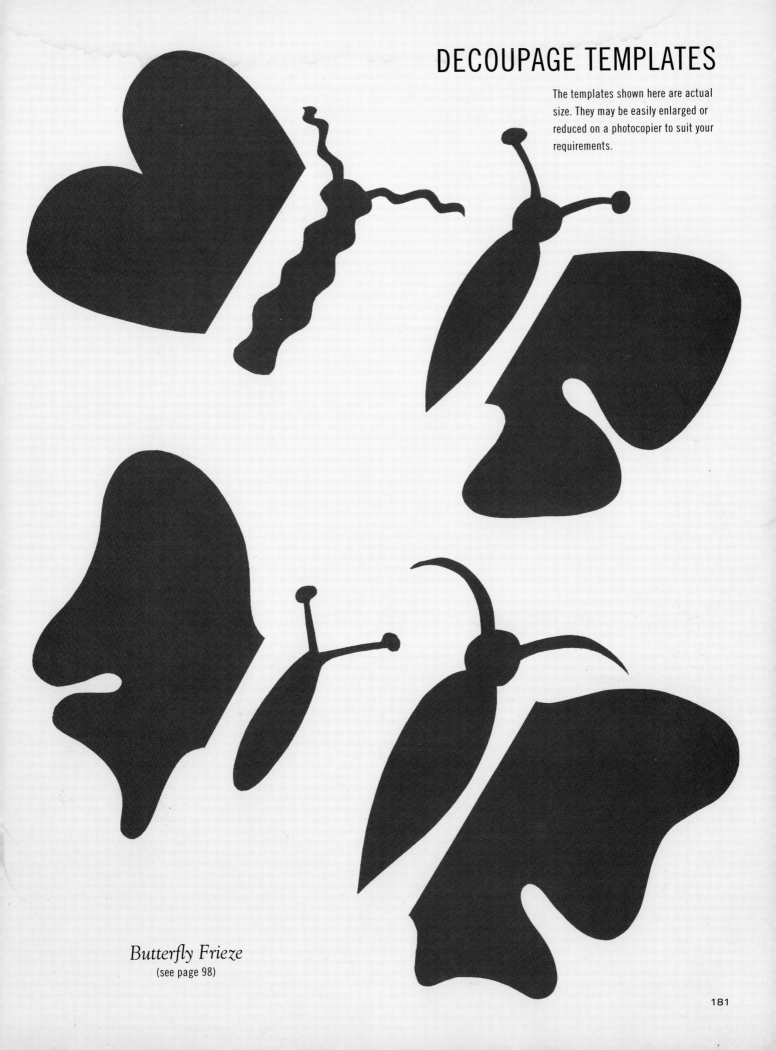

# DECOUPAGE TEMPLATES

The templates shown here are actual size. They may be easily enlarged or reduced on a photocopier to suit your requirements.

*Butterfly Frieze*
(see page 98)

*Stars and Circles
Roller Blind*
(see page 77)

*Black Cat Lamp and Shade*
(see page 92)

# PAINTING GLASS TEMPLATES

The templates shown here are actual size.
They may be easily enlarged or reduced on a
photocopier to suit the size of the glass to
be decorated.

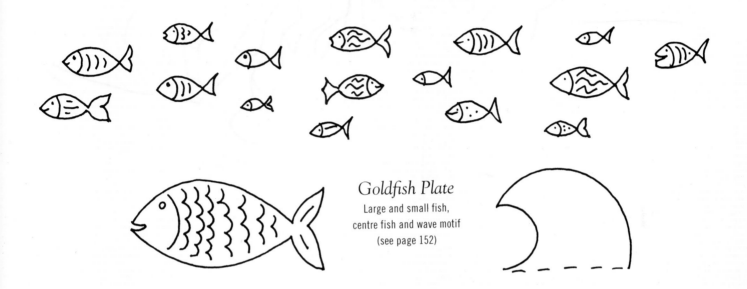

### Goldfish Plate

Large and small fish,
centre fish and wave motif
(see page 152)

### Olive Oil Bottle

Olive spray (see page 143)

### Leaf and Tendril design

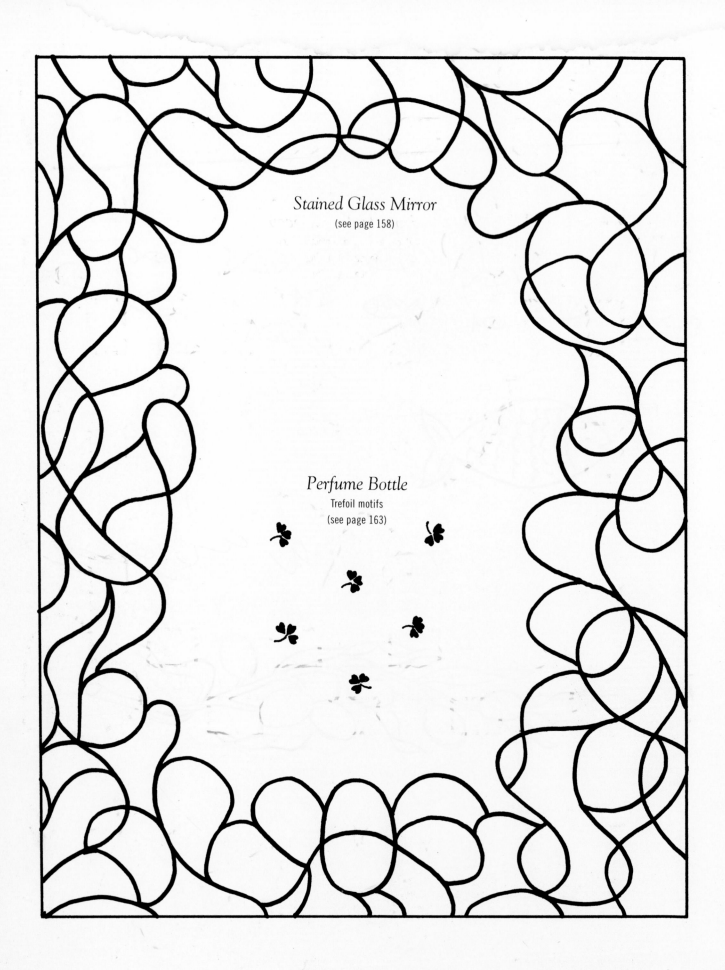

Stained Glass Mirror
(see page 158)

Perfume Bottle
Trefoil motifs
(see page 163)

### Frosted Glass Window
Cockerel, heart and blocks pattern
for stencil making
(see page 166)

### Starry Oil Burner
Star shapes (see page 160)

*Floral Roundels*
(see page 172)

*Floral Border*
(use this design to
decorate the corners of
mirrors or clip frames)

*Getting started heart stencil design*
(see page 147)

# SUPPLIERS

## UNITED KINGDOM

Fred Aldous
37 Lever Street
Manchester M1 1LW
Tel: 0161 236 2477
Fax: 0161 236 6075
(*Wide range of craft
products. Mail order*)

Cake Art Ltd
Venture Way
Crown Estate
Priorswood
Taunton
Somerset TA2 8DE
Tel: 0182 332 1532
(*General cake decorating
supplies*)

Craft Creations
Ingersoll House
Delamare Road
Cheshunt
Herts EN8 9ND
Tel: 01992 781 900

Clearcraft
Unit 44
Leyton Industrial Village
Argall Avenue
London E10 7QP
Tel: 020 8539 9015
(*Oil burners shown on
page 157, 160*)

Servicepoint UK
Landore Court
46 Charles Street
Cardiff CF1 4ED
Tel: 01222 664 420
(*General art suppliers*)

The English Stamp Co.
Sunnydown
Worth Matravers
Dorset BH19 3JP
Tel: 01929 439117
(*Stamps, stamping paint
and rollers*)

Egyptian House
Unit A2, Hatcham
  Mews Business Centre
Hatcham Park Road
London SE14 1QN
Tel: 020 7732 4321
(*Coloured glassware; mail
order and wholesale only*)

Emmaus UK
4 Salisbury Villas
Station Road
Cambridge CB1 2JF
Tel: 01223 863 657
(*Second-hand glassware*)

Falkiner Fine Papers Ltd.
76 Southampton Row
London WC1B 4AR
Tel: 020 7831 1151

Heffers Art & Graphics
15-21 King Street
Cambridge CB1 1LH
Tel: 01223 568495
(*Painting and drawing
materials*)

Inca Stamp
136 Stanley Green Road
Poole
Dorset BH15 3AH
Tel: 01202 777 222
(*Stamps, rollers and
embossing powder*)

Liquitex Paints
Binney and Smith
(Eur.) Ltd
Ampthill Road
Bedford MK42 9RS
Tel: 01234 360201
(*Paints*)

John Mathieson & Co
48 Frederick Street
Edinburgh EH2 1EX
Tel: 0131 225 6798
(*General art suppliers*)

Moira Neal
5 Barrowcrofts
Histon
Cambridge CB4 4EU
(*Dough making day
schools; send sae*)

Panduro Hobby Ltd
Westway House
Transport Avenue
Brentford
Middlesex TW8 9HF
Tel: 020 8847 6161
(*Pébéo paints and other
crafts supplies. Mail
order*)

Paperchase
213 Tottenham Court Rd
London W1P 9AF
Tel: 020 7580 8496
or
St Mary's Gate
Manchester
Tel: 0161 839 1500
(*Decorative papers; check
for your local branch*)

Philip & Tacey Ltd
North Way
Andover
Hampshire SP10 5BA
Tel: 01264 332171
(*Pébéo glass paints, fabric
stamps and paints, crackle
and patinating varnish*)

Polyvine Ltd.
Vine House
Rockhampton
Berkeley
Glos. GL13 9DT
Tel: 01454 261276
(*Crackle glaze, crackle
varnish, and a variety of
other decorative paint
finishes*)

J F Renshaw Ltd
Crown Street
Liverpool L8 7RF
Tel: 0151 706 8200
(*General cake decorating
supplies*)

Specialist Crafts Ltd
Homecrafts Direct
P.O. Box 38
Leicester LE1 9BU
Tel: (0116) 251 3139
Fax: (0116) 251 5015
(*Wide range of craft
materials. Mail order*)

Karin Van Heerden
PO Box 558
Oxford OX1 5AJ
(*Cat papers as used on
page 106, available by
mail order*)

### Flower Crafts Suppliers

The Herbal Apothecary
103 High Street, Syston
Leicester LE7 1GQ
Tel: 0116 260 2690

The Hop Shop
Castle Farm
Shoreham, Sevenoaks
Kent TN14 7UB
Tel: 01959 523 219

Terence Moore Designs
The Barn Workshop
Burleigh Lane
Crawley Down
West Sussex RH10 4LF
Tel: 01342 717 944

Veevers Carter
The Chelsea Gardener
Unit 10, East Building
Westminster Business
  Square
1-45 Durham Street
London SE11 5JH
Tel: 020 7735 1400

Silk Landscapes
164 Old Brompton Rd.
London SW5 OBA
Tel: 020 7835 1500

Fast Flowers Ltd
609 Fulham Road
London SW6 5UA
Tel: 020 7381 6422

## SOUTH AFRICA

Anne's Arts and Crafts
6 Recreation Road
Fish Hoek, Cape Town
Tel: 021 782 2061/
782 3169
Fax: 021 782 6268

Art Leather and
Handcraft
Shop 107
Musgrave Centre
124 Musgrave Road
Durban
Tel: 031 21 9517

Art Mates
Shop 313
Musgrave Centre
124 Musgrave Road
Durban
Tel: 031 21 0094

Auckland Park
  Floral Boutique
7 Seventh Street
Melville
Johannesburg 2092
Tel: 011 726 2116

Baking Tin
Bloemfontein
051 481 433
Cape Town 021 61 6434
East London 0431 56175
George 0441 74 6082
Port Elizabeth
041 334 051
Randburg 011 792 8189

Corner Arts and Crafts
52 4th Avenue
Newton Park
Port Elizabeth
Tel: 0431 57 231

The Craftsman
Shop 10
Progress House
110 Bordeaux Drive
Randburg
Tel: 011 787 1846

Crafty Supplies
32 Main Road
Claremeont
Cape Town
Tel: 021 61 0308

Franken
445 Hilda Street
Hatfield
Pretoria
Tel: 011 43 6414

Hiningklip Dry Flowers
13 Lady Anne Avenue
Newlands
Cape Town 770
Tel: 021 64 4410

L & P Stationery and
　Artists' Requirements
65b Church Street
Bloemfontein
Tel: 051 30 3061

Mycrafts Shop
Aliwal Street
Bloemfontein
Tel: 051 48 4119

Peers Handicrafts
35 Burg Street
Cape Town
Tel: 021 24 2520

Polyflora
8 January Road
Bloemfontein
Tel: 051 34 1371

PW Story (Pty) Ltd.
18 Foundry Lane
Durban
Tel: 031 306 1224

E Schweikerdt (Pty) Ltd
475 Fehren Street
Pretoria
Tel: 021 46 5406
Mail Order Service
PO Box 697
Pretoria 0001

Southern Arts and
　Crafts
105 Main Road
Rosettenville,
Johannesburg
Tel/Fax: 011 683 6566

AUSTRALIA

Arts & Crafts Corner
34 Mint Street
East Victoria Park
WA 6101
Tel: 08 9361 4567

Boronia Arts &
　Crafts Centre
247 Dorset Road
Boronia
VIC 3155
Tel: 03 9762 1751

Cake and Icing Centre
651 Samford Road
Mitchelton
QLD 4053
Tel: 07 3355 3443

Cake Decorating Centre
1 Adelaide Arcade
Adelaide
SA 5000
Tel: 08 8223 1719

The Craft Crowd
Shop 60 Sunnybank
　Plaza
Main Road
Sunnybank
QLD 4109
Tel: 07 3345 9812

Craft Lovers
46 Murray Street
Tanunda
SA 5352
Tel: 08 8563 1133

Dominion Agencies
20 Stuart Road
Dulwich
SA 5065
Tel: 08 8332 6144

Flowerama
Unit 27
8 Gladstone Road
Castle Hill
NSW 2154
Tel: 02 9680 2320

Flower World
12 Sara Grove
Tottenham
VIC 3012
Tel: 03 9315 2388

Finishing Touches Cake
　Decorating Centre
268 Centre Road
Bentleigh
VIC 3204
Tel: 03 9557 9099

Hobbytex
5 Victoria Avenue
Castle Hill
NSW 2154
Tel: 02 9634 5388

Lincraft
Gallery Level
Imperial Arcade
Pitt Street
Sydney
NSW 2000
Tel: 02 9221 5111

Oxford Art Supplies
221-223 Oxford Street
Darlinghurst
NSW 2010
Tel: 02 9360 4066

Petersen's Cake
　Decorations
Rear 698 Beaufort Street
Mt Lawley
WA 6050
Tel: 08 9271 1692

Timbertop Nursery
1387 Wanneroo Road
Wanneroo
WA 6065
Tel: 08 9306 3398

NEW ZEALAND

Allen's Rubber Stamps
PO Box 283
Warkworth
Tel/Fax: 09 357 0412

Auckland Flower
　Wholesalers Ltd
388 Church St.
Penrose
Tel: 09 579 5692

Auckland Folk Art
　Centre
591 Remuera Road
Upland Village
Auckland
Tel: 09 524 0936

Auckland Rubber Stamps
Unit 2
50 Stoddard Road
Mt Roskill, Auckland
Tel: 09 629 2692

Colleen Murphy Florists
119 Akitchener Road
Milford Square
Tel: 09 489 5961

Draw Art Supplies Ltd
5 Mahunga Drive
Mangere Bridge
Auckland
Tel: 09 636 4862

Dominion Paint Centre
227 Dominion Road
Mt Eden, Auckland
Tel: 0800 555 959

Expression Flower Shop
359 Gt North Road
Henderson
Tel: 09 836 5068

Flower Systems Ltd
8 Macklehurst Road
Auckland
Tel: 09 337 4515

Headerish Flowers
Shirley
Christchurch
Tel: 0800 50 505

Interflora
Head Office
Tel: 0800 80 88 80
(Branches nationwide)

Golden Bridge
　Marketing Ltd
Cake Decorating
　Supplies
Cnr Ride Way &
William Pickering Drive
Albany
Tel: 09 373 3492

P A Inkman Ltd
36 Douglas Street
Ponsonby
Auckland
Tel: 09 638 7593

Palmers Gardenworld
44 Khuber Pass Rd
Auckland
Tel: 09 302 0400

The Partners
St Martins Stationary
5 Austin-Kirk Lane
Christchurch 2
(General craft supplies)

The Reumuera Florist
319 Reumuera Road
Auckland
Tel: 09 520 8379

Studio Art Supplies
225 Parnell Road
Parnell
Auckland
Tel: 09 377 0302

# INDEX